Burkholder, Byron

They Saw His Glory

DATE DUE

they saw his glory

stories of conversion and service

edited by
byron burkholder

Kindred Press

WINNIPEG, MB, CANADA   HILLSBORO, KS, U.S.A.

TABLE OF CONTENTS

FOREWORD

What does the good news of Jesus mean to a black tailor in Colombia's Chocó lowlands? How does it change the life of a mother in the modern city of Osaka, Japan? Why is it revolutionary in the work of a nonliterate Bible woman in India, or a rural pastor in Zaire? *They Saw His Glory* contains some glimpses of answers.

This is a book of stories about Christians in eleven countries where North American Mennonite Brethren have served during the last few decades. Through the years, churches in these countries have come into their own. Their members have experienced the transforming gospel which cuts across the economic, social and cultural barriers which divide today's world.

They Saw His Glory provides an opportunity for North Americans to become acquainted with these sisters and brothers. Admittedly, the book contains only a tiny sampling of all the stories that have been told, both orally and in writing. However, we have tried to make it representative of as many age groups, economic circumstances and religious backgrounds as possible, thus demonstrating the breadth of the Christian community around the world.

Those who participated in the writing of these stories under the sponsorship of Mennonite Brethren Missions/Services were profoundly affected by the bond of fellowship which developed as their overseas brothers and sisters shared their lives with them. We hope that this volume will spark in readers something of the same bond, and a renewed vision of the grace of God in the lives of his people around the world.

Byron Burkholder, ed.

ACKNOWLEDGEMENTS

The stories in *They Saw His Glory* emerge out of a series of volunteer writing/research assignments under Mennonite Brethren Missions/Services, during 1982-83. In the late summer of 1982 *Frieda Esau* and *Carolyn Hamm* of Winnipeg, Manitoba, travelled to Asia for a 10 month stint in India, Indonesia and Japan. Both are graduates of the University of Winnipeg. Frieda, who hails from Coaldale, Alberta, is currently finishing a master's program in history at the University of Winnipeg. Carolyn, who was born in India to Mennonite Brethren missionaries, is completing teacher's training at the University of Manitoba.

John and Christine Longhurst, also of Winnipeg, spent the same fall and winter in Germany, Austria and Spain, with a short trip to Mexico afterwards. John is now staff writer for Mennonite Central Committee (Canada), while Christine is juggling a part-time job as secretary with MBM/S and music teaching and conducting. Both are graduates of Mennonite Brethren Bible College and the University of Winnipeg.

In the spring and summer of 1983, three more volunteers offered their writing skills to MBM/S. *Cheryl Martin* of Fresno, California, worked in Brazil for several weeks alongside *Adrienne Wiebe* of Edmonton, Alberta. Wiebe, who is currently finishing a Master's degree in Geography at the University of Alberta, then went on to Uruguay and Paraguay. Meanwhile, Cheryl joined *Frances Martens* in Colombia. Frances, a graduate of Goshen College (Indiana) returned home to Fresno, California, to take teacher's training at Fresno Pacific College. Cheryl, a graduate of Pacific, accepted a two-year assignment as a writer/researcher with Mennonite Central Committee's Peace Section in Washington, D.C.

Also in the summer of 1983, the editor, *Byron Burkholder,* took a four-month leave from his work as MBM/S information services director to travel and write in Africa and South

America, focussing mainly on Zaire. Born in Ethiopia to Mennonite medical missionaries, Byron is a graduate of York University, Ontario.

Finally, thanks go to *Ray Dirks* for the cover design and the inside illustrations. Dirks, a professional artist from Vancouver, B.C., is serving with his wife Katie in a short-term MBM/S assignment in Kinshasa, Zaire.

Frieda Esau

Carolyn Hamm

Cheryl Martin

Adrienne Wiebe

Frances Martens

Byron Burkholder

John & Christine Longhurst

india

INDIA

Population: 684 million
Capital: New Delhi
Languages: Hindi, English and 14 other official
              languages
Religions: Hindu (83%), Muslim (11%), Christian
              (2.6%), Sikh, Jain, Buddhist. (Evangelicals:
              0.4%)

Mennonite Brethren Conference in India: over 25,000 members, 700 village groups.

Missions/Services ministries: Bible teaching, church planting, Muslim evangelism, broadcasting.

India was the first country to capture the vision of North American Mennonite Brethren. Ten years after Abram and Mary Friesen of Russia started work among the Telugu-speaking people in 1890, the foreign mission board in North America appointed its first missionary team to serve in the same area. After the turn of the century, medical and educational programs flourished, and the church was built. In the 1960's the mission was working in 10 fields in Andhra Pradesh state.

Since 1968 the Mennonite Brethren church has been administratively responsible for all church and institutional programs. This has meant greater indigenization at all levels, and a decline in the size of the missionary staff. The church has continued to grow through considerable local evangelistic initiative; moreover, the church has largely overcome the division which overshadowed the conference in 1978-81.

P. Moses

As dawn was breaking, the little group of Christians outside the village stared at each other dumbfounded. Garlands of money were being placed around their necks amid the loud cheers of an excited crowd! Seldom had a band of preachers been so well received.

Their leader, P. Moses, seemed unaware of the great honor being shown to them. Instead, his eyes were scanning the crowd for signs of a deeper response from the people. Since the previous evening the crowd had been watching these Christians perform a popular Indian musical drama, the *Bahjan*. Traditionally, a *Bahjan* celebrates the epics of Hindu gods and heroes, but this time it had related the gospel message.

In his quiet, unassuming way, Moses had again launched out into a new method of ministry to Hindu people. If this crowd's response was an indication of how it would be received, the prospects were better than he had ever hoped for. His face lit up as his vision slowly took shape again. If he could do his part in spreading the message, God would do the rest.

Moses had always worked toward goals he believed in. As a young man, he had been the first one in his family to give up laboring in the fields around the small village where he lived in order to learn the art of performing *Bahjans*. Surrounding himself images and pictures of Hindu deities for inspiration, he struggled to perfect himself in the art. His goal: to become a guru and teach the skill to others.

His determination paid off. Soon he was travelling from village to village, attracting little groups of followers. By spreading the classic Hindu tales, he was fighting to revive Hinduism among the common people.

One day Moses received an invitation to come and teach his *Bahjans* to the members of a Christian community. Accepting their invitation, he found himself in touch with a new kind of people. Although they were diligent students during the week, they had a strange habit of leaving the learning of *Bahjans* every Sunday to attend church services.

Not knowing how to deal with disciples who deserted their master once a week, Moses' curiosity compelled him to follow them to church. It was here that he first heard of Jesus Christ.

About the same time, the local pastor was also becoming concerned about the lack of commitment in his own community. The interest in Moses and his Hindu *Bahjans* prompted the pastor to start a series of evangelistic meetings. Here, the evangelist's message touched Moses deeply and he sensed a change taking place in his heart.

One day, while out in the hills collecting firewood, Moses was suddenly stung by a scorpion. Suffering from one of the most painful of all poisonous insect stings, he tried chanting *mantras* to relieve the pain. They didn't work. Then he remembered a Christian song he had heard which spoke of God giving help in times of need. He started singing as much as he could remember and pleaded with God. "If you will relieve the pain, I will dedicate my life to you," he promised. At once he had relief.

Moses held fast to that promise. He is now a pastor working among the Telugu-speaking people of Mennonite Brethren background who have moved out of Andhra Pradesh, the state where the Mennonite Brethren church has existed since the first missionaries came. Five years ago, a

14

church in the state of Karnataka was established as a result of Moses' work.

Since the early 1950s when a huge dam project was begun in Karnataka, people of Mennonite Brethren background had been migrating to the area in hopes of finding jobs as contract laborers. They lived in the tattered shacks and mud huts characteristic of laborers' camps, trying to preserve their Telugu language and their denominational heritage.

When Moses arrived in 1974, he found a group of people in desperate need of spiritual leadership. Moving into a one-room, thatch-roofed, mud hut, Moses and his family became a part of them.

Now there are five Mennonite Brethren churches in the area, but the need for leadership is still great. With only one co-worker, Moses pastors all five of the churches, travelling to each of them on a given day each week to hold services. He also visits twenty additional village communities working to plant more churches.

Starting churches is only one part of the vision, however. From his own experience, Moses knows that it is also important to keep the church faithful to its calling. When he became a Christian he taught himself to read and write so that he could better discover the truths of Scripture. He initiated Bible studies and prayer meetings in order to share his faith. He even gave up the *Bahjans* that he had spent so many years learning.

While the people around him were impressed by his zeal, they seemed to be trying to dissuade him. They said, ''You'll grow out of it. We also accepted the Christian faith when the first missionaries came and we left everything to follow them, but it was meaningless. You will be just like us one of these days.''

Refusing to believe them, yet hampered in his ministry by them, Moses was soon overcome with mental and physical exhaustion. During the lengthy illness which resulted, he suffered through periods of unconsciousness in which he would see black ghostly forms standing over him. As he lay helpless, frightening creatures with wild hair and terrifying eyes would attack him.

Then it was his Hindu neighbors who mocked him. "What kind of new faith do you have?" they taunted. "It seems your God is helpless. In your condition he should come and help you regain your good health. We are not Christians, but we are healthy. We must be better than you."

For two long years, Moses suffered persecution from both Hindus and "Christians," but he never gave up. He only continued to pray. Eventually, his tormentors lost interest and their mocking died down, but Moses remained faithful. His leadership of small groups soon excelled and he was recommended for Bible school. Today, having completed that training, Moses is encountering many needs among the people he serves in Karnataka. One of them is the need of basic education. Moses longs to develop the potential in the many little children who loiter around the laborers' camps. The children, in turn, are already enjoying his leadership in Sunday school programs. With bright smiles, happy voices and clapping hands, they enthusiastically follow along. "We need to find ways and means by which we can teach them," Moses claims. "Even just a small school where they can learn to read and write and get a little more Christian education."

In one sense, Moses seems to be asking very little. Yet his vision is impressive and the goals he has set are high. Even as a church building is now going up, he continues to plan for its future. Located at the edge of the main market place in the large town of Gangavati, the new church has been designed to allow an additional level. Thus, the building will prominently rise above the structures around it, a witness to the world and a monument to the vision of a leader who is faithful in the service of his Lord.

Carolyn Hamm

Karnamma

Through the villages she goes, leading women's Bible studies, giving advice, answering questions and teaching songs and verses. Karnamma is a Bible woman for the Mennonite Brethren Church in India. While touring villages south of Hyderabad, she ministers primarily to women and children. Her concern for them rises from her own experience of the pressures that a new Christian, and specifically a woman convert, faces in India.

Formerly a devout Hindu, Karnamma knows well the basic teaching of Hinduism, that even if there are as many as 33 million incarnations, God is one. But while worshipping family gods, village gods and personal gods, Karnamma couldn't help asking, "Which one?" She finds others asking the same question. "I want them to know how God showed me that he is the one and only God," she says.

From a shepherd caste family in the village of Shadnager, Karnamma was taught from childhood that to please God, she had to worship the gods devotedly. There were many idols in her home, and she would do **puja** (worship) daily by offering coconut, incense, flowers or fruit. With nonliterate parents, Karnamma never received any systematic teaching about Hinduism, but from her family she learned about the god Venkateshwara and about the Hindu trinity: Vishnu, Shiva and Brahma. By observing others in the village, she learned about Hanuman the monkey god, Ganesh the elephant god, and about Kali and Durga, the fierce goddesses of war and destruction. Some gods Karnamma "inherited," for they were specific to her family, her caste and her village. There were gods and goddesses of fire, of fertility, of wisdom, of cholera and of smallpox. Worshipping and pleasing them was a very serious concern.

When Karnamma was only 10 years old, she was promised to a man whom her parents had chosen for her soon after she was born. But before she had met her husband, he died, leaving Karnamma a widow at age 16. Her husband's death had a great impact upon her. She began to wonder about the meaning of life, and asked, "What happens after we die? Is there life? Is there a future? My desire was that I could worship my creator and enter into *Moksha* (paradise). But first I wanted to know who my creator was." Karnamma noticed how carefully her sister-in-law observed the Hindu festivals of Sravanamasum and Shivaratri by practising many rituals and fasting and praying. She began to think, "Perhaps if I worhsip more sincerely I will know my creator."

Before long, she was rivalling even her sister-in-law in Hindu devotion. She kept the rituals carefully, celebrating Shivaratri and joining in the vigorous fasting. Because they were not to sleep during certain festivals, many people would stay awake by going on pilgrimages to certain villages, where they would spend their time with singing, worship and meditation. "But we poorer people couldn't travel like that," says Karnamma. "So I used to sit at home and worship. Sometimes my sister-in-law would sleep, but I was afraid to. With a small lamp and a book, I struggled to stay awake, so that God would honor me and grant my desire."

One Friday, as she was preparing to worship Vishnu, her personal god, she heard a visitor enter her house. She put down the brass offering tray she was washing to greet an old Brahmin priest who came by on occasion to give medicine to her parents. From each person he visited, he would collect monthly or yearly offerings, usually gifts of money, or of rice, vegetables or fruit. Karnamma had seen housewives, merchants and tradesmen place gifts in the Brahmin's hands, then bow down to touch his feet in a gesture of devotion.

When she saw the priest, Karnamma thought, "Here is an important man with much religious knowledge and influence. I will ask him about my doubts. Surely from him I will get a good answer." So she asked the man, "Sir, we have so many idols. Are they real? Is Vishnu really God?" To her great disappointment the old man answered, "It is only to satisfy our spiritual hunger that we worship these images. The only god is Yakonaryana (meaning literally, 'God is one'). The rest is just for our own satisfaction."

"What a disappointing moment that was in my life," says Karnamma. "I had been worshipping so sincerely, but now I began to think, 'Maybe my worship of Vishnu is a waste. There is a god greater than Vishnu that I should be worshipping.' From that time, outwardly I would worship Vishnu, but inwardly I wanted to discover and worship a greater god. I wanted to know Yakonaryana, the greatest and only god."

"Although I didn't know the scriptures at that time," says Karnamma, "now I believe that even before the foundations of this world were laid, God had chosen me and given me a desire to know him."

Christianity was almost unknown to Karnamma. Only vaguely does she remember a day when a missionary lady and an Indian evangelist visited her village to share about the crucifixion of Christ and his sufferings for humanity. At that time she thought, "How could a god suffer? And why would he suffer?"

Karnamma describes the day when her questions were answered and her desire to know God was fulfilled: "While I was studying at a school near my village. I would often stay for the night at the house of my grandmother. All of my school books were in the Urdu language, and one day I searched the shelves of my grandmother's house for books in my own Telugu langugae. One in particular caught my eye—a Christian book entitled *Murkti Margum* (Way to Salvation).

"As I read the book I learned about the creation of the universe and of man. In Hinduism no one had ever answered my question of 'Who was my creator?' Until that day I had thought that the Christian God was just another great guru. But I came to discover that he is much more than that—he is the creator of this whole universe and the creator of me.

"I was surprised to read about man as a sinner because I had never been taught about sin before. Even though I had only a little education, I clearly understood the message I read in Isaiah 53:6, that all like sheep have gone astray. I began to see that I too was lost; while all of us were worshipping our personal deities, we had gone astray from worshipping the real creator. This became as clear as if someone was sitting beside me and explaining all these things. I knew that I was far away from my creator.

"I discovered . . . why Christ suffered. He suffered to save me. It was only when I repented of my evil deeds and told God that I wanted to worship and serve him alone, that I felt relieved of my burden. I felt an inexpressible joy."

From that day 30 years ago, Karnamma wanted to live as a Christian according to God's word. But because she was a widow, she was supposed to stay under the protection of her mother and brother who were the heads of the family while her father was away. She was not only to live with them but also to obey them. Afraid to tell her mother of her decision to follow Christ, she used to pray every day in secret.

"In the book of Acts the Ethiopian 'heard and believed,' " notes Karnamma. "I never thought that this could happen to my mother." But one day as she and her mother were at the well drawing water, they met two village women returning from a Christian prayer service held in a nearby village. The women were excited about the meeting and invited Karnamma's mother to attend. Out of curiosity, she decided to go. When a preacher there spoke about Jesus Christ, she instantly believed this teaching to be true, and it was not long before she too had committed her life to Christ. Karnamma contacted a Mennonite Brethren preacher in a nearby village, and he made arrangements for Karnamma and her mother to be baptized at the mission compound at Shamshabad.

"After I was baptized," says Karnamma, "no one told me to share about my conversion and about Christ, but I had a desire, an inner voice which gave me the courage and a burden to share the gospel. Before, I was too cowardly and shy to do so. But after my baptism I would tell all the people who came to visit at our house. Wherever I would go, whether in the train, the bus, or the bullock cart, and whatever I was doing, I would share about Christ."

In Karnamma's house were pictures of Hindu gods. She took these down and replaced them with pictures showing the whole life story of Christ—his birth, his ministry, his death and resurrection. Whenever visitors would see the picture of the crucifixion they would ask, "Who is this man? Why is he being killed?" Then Karnamma would tell the story.

From a Mennonite Brethren missionary, Miss Helen Harder (now Loewen), Karnamma used to collect tracts, which she would read before passing them to others. She and her mother were regularly seen carrying Bibles on their way to prayer fellowships and church services. They removed all the idols from their house, and no longer attended the Hindu festival celebrations. The news spread throughout the village that they had changed their faith.

People began to react differently to them. Karnamma explains, "When we would go to the well to draw water, we would notice that the people drawing water after us would first ritually clean the well. They considered us unclean and did not want to be affected by our presence. Although they didn't accuse or confront us at first, we could tell that they gossiped about us amongst themselves.

"The whole community would often meet together and have discussions about us," says Karnamma. "They threatened to excommunicate me if I would not deny Christ. Later, they threatened me further saying, 'Not only you, but your mother, your brother and your whole family will be excommunicated if you will not worship our gods.'" But Karnamma replied, "If you must excommunicate us, do so. But I will not leave Christ."

In 1957 Karnamma was banned from her village. With no place to go, she came to the Shamshabad Bible School where missionary principal J.J. Dick encouraged her to get training for the ministry. After graduating from the three-year course, she worked at the school for a time, serving as teacher and matron for the women students.

Since that time Karnamma has served as a Bible woman. She has a vital ministry among caste women, many of whom have become Christians through her testimony. She encourages them in their Christian lives, for many of them are afraid to face their families or oppose their husbands and age-old tradition by renouncing Hinduism. One woman says she will become a Christian after all her children are married. She is afraid to jeopardize opportunities to find husbands for her daughters. Another hesitates to stop wearing a *butu* (Hindu mark) on her forehead. Others are afraid to remove the idols and pictures of Hindu gods from their homes.

In one home Karnamma noticed that behind a picture of a Hindu god was a picture of Christ. The couple living there were secret believers who were continuing their worship of Hindu gods for the sake of their neighbors. They feared that if they openly professed Christianity, no one would allow them to rent property, and they would be left homeless.

Karnamma understands the pressures faced by new Christians, especially those coming from villages in which Christianity is new. She knows how difficult it is for a first generation Christian in India to step out of the tightly-interdependent village community and exchange security for rejection. Nevertheless, Karnamma keeps on teaching others to be not only hearers of the Word but doers also. She can teach this because she knows from experience the power which commands obedience and overcomes fears.

Frieda Esau

B. Nathaniel

"I was born a Hindu," B. Nathaniel says. "But even when I was a devotee I really didn't know what it was about."

Like countless others in India, the elderly man was born to nonliterate parents, in the village of Ippukuntha. From them he inherited the label "outcaste" and the accompanying social stigma, customs and lifestyle. Nathaniel learned most of what he knew of Hinduism by observing and imitating his parents. "For instance," he says, "If they would worship a certain image then I would too. If they would break coconut or offer rice and incense, then I would do the same."

From an early age he was also aware of where he stood in the social ranking of the caste-conscious society. He noticed how an orthodox highcaste person would not eat food prepared by an outcaste, draw water from the same well, or sometimes even allow the shadow of an outcaste person to cross his path.

But over the years, Nathaniel has not been bound by the restrictions of caste. Today he is a devout and respected Christian pastor in India's Mennonite Brethren Church. He is known for the way he boldly stands up for what he has found to be true, and for the way he speaks of this truth to everyone he meets, regardless of their caste or position.

When he was a young boy, Nathaniel's parents were concerned that he receive an education; he was the only son in the family. So they applied to the school at the Nagarkurnool Mennonite Brethren mission compound several miles away, where many of Nathaniel's friends were attending. There, besides the regular courses, Nathaniel learned about a God other than the ones he had grown up with. When he questioned his parents about this God, he found that they too had been listening to the teaching of the Christians in the area. Nathaniel's parents had accepted Christ as one among their many other gods; so their son did the same.

While Nathaniel was attending the Nagarkurnool school, his family and elders began to encourage him to be baptized. With their limited knowledge they said to him, "Look, the other boys your age are all being baptized. If you are baptized, then you will be saved and have a joyful life." Nathaniel took this advice and joined the others in baptism. Again, there was more imitation than understanding.

In fact, his baptism was only the beginning of a long struggle. "I wanted to know for certain who God was," he says. "I knew Jesus was not just another like the many Hindu gods which some people worship so devotedly. But how could I know which was true?"

Finally Nathaniel came to test the claims of the Hindu religion. Near his home was a hill called Omar Mahishveri. The local Hindu people believe that if a righteous person goes onto the hill, rain will fall on him. But if a wicked person goes, the rain will surely not fall. Nathaniel longed to visit that place to see whether or not it would proclaim him righteous. Finally one day he gathered his courage and approached the hill. He noticed that a woman notorious for her evil deeds was climbing the hill just before him. What a shock it was for Nathaniel to see the rain falling on her. When he got to the top of the hill, again the rain fell. "It was then," he says, "that I realized it could not be true. I knew I was wicked and a sinner inside, yet there was rain. I was very troubled. Where was the truth?"

Nathaniel continued his search. One night, he prayed fervently, "Lord, if you are real, please reveal yourself to me.

Show me who you are." Then he slept. At about four o'clock in the morning, he woke up suddenly when he heard his name being called. "Nathaniel, Nathaniel, Nathaniel. Get up, light your lamp and read Psalm 46." Obediently he read the words, "Cease striving and know that I am God; I will be exalted among the nations, I will be exalted on earth." After reading the passage, Nathaniel says, "there came a joy and peace in my heart, because I now believed that Jesus was the only living savior. And he had saved me."

In the same way that he had tested out the claims of the Hindu religion, Nathaniel dared to test God's promises. One day, after reading in Mark 13:9, "You shall be brought before governors and kings as a testimony for my sake," Nathaniel prayed, "Lord, I am an ordinary man. Do you mean that I could stand before important and high caste people in Nagarkurnool?" He heard God's reply, "Yes, go."

Immediately Nathaniel took a bicycle rickshaw to the home of a reputable doctor in the town. He explains, "I simply told him I had come to visit and pray with him. I did pray, and then I told him about Christ. The doctor ended up asking me for a Bible. I was impressed that God could use me in that way."

Nathaniel attended the Mennonite Brethren Bible Institute in Shamshabad with his wife and family before joining the Mennonite Brethren "preachers' list" in India, currently numbering about 150. With an estimated 28,000 M.B. Christians scattered in about 750 villages, the preachers have to travel in village circuits. As a village circuit leader for the past 15 years, Nathaniel pastors one church and serves people in a cluster of neighboring villages as well. An assistant preacher helps him cover 24 villages in the Nagarkurnool "field," one of the nine districts south of Hyderabad in which the Mennonite Brethren mission used to have stations.

B. Nathaniel continues to speak to "governors and kings." One day as he was speaking to tribal people in a forest area, he was surrounded by a group of officials—a police lieutenant, a district official and others. They had come to arrest him saying that he was preaching in a prohibited area.

As they took him down the road, one of the officials asked Nathaniel, "Why do you want to preach that Christ is the only God? Is Rama not a god?" Nathaniel was somewhat hesitant to answer. If he said that only Jesus was Lord, the devout Hindu man would consider the reply blasphemous. These were educated and powerful men. What could he say? He prayed to God for an answer. Then he carefully replied, "Sir, you, an important and intelligent man, are worshipping Rama. You should be able to tell me whether or not he is a god."

The man became very angry. He shouted at Nathaniel and threatened that he would send him far away to a jail. Nathaniel replied, "If you send me there, I will preach to everyone I meet so they too will hear the word of God." The official fumed, "If you insist on preaching, then I will give a black card about you to every police station saying that you are a criminal."

Nathaniel responded, "If you give me a black card here on earth, I will get a red card in heaven where my Lord will honor me." Finally the official said, "I don't want to talk to you now. Go from here." So Nathaniel went on his way. He went to the village and preached the gospel.

Frieda Esau

J. Pavani

J. Pavani is a young Indian woman studying at the Mennonite Brethren Bible Institute in Shamshabad, 12 miles south of the city of Hyderabad. Here is her testimony, as told to Carolyn Hamm:

I was born and brought up in a Hindu family in the city of Guntur. When I was a child, my parents taught me to worship idols in the traditional ways and I used to think the images were gods. Even so, our religion was more of a ritual than a faith.

Although my parents were devout Hindus, it was through them that I first learned about Jesus Christ. Here is how it came about: In India, it is very important to have boys in the family, but we had only girls. Every time my mother gave birth to a baby boy it would die. So the village priest started conducting special religious ceremonies to try to stop the male children from dying, but they never worked.

Then my father heard about a Christian prayer meeting and as a last resort, my parents went. There the preacher prayed for my mother and by the grace of God, my brother is still alive. This impressed my parents so much that they began to worship Jesus as well as all their Hindu gods.

Later, I studied in a Christian convent school. I also listened to the gospel message on the radio, especially the Trans World Radio broadcasts. The preacher used to emphasize that Jesus is the only Lord and that he must be a

28

personal Savior. This voice challenged me to think seriously about it. Finally, at the age of 17, I accepted Jesus Christ as my Saviour.

But when I asked my mother and father about being baptized, they would not hear of it. They said I was too young to think of such things and since I was a girl I should be careful. Besides, it would be difficult for them to arrange a good marriage for me if I were a Christian. So I had to postpone my baptism.

Then one Christmas, a nearby Christian church was having a special party and I went. Afterwards, a preacher got up and asked if there were any who wanted to be baptized. The Spirit of the Lord was moving in my heart, so I raised my hand. Later, as I talked with the preacher, my sister tried to stop me. "Be careful," she warned, "You are a Hindu girl. You will have a Hindu marriage and will have to worship Hindu gods. Please don't take baptism."

But the preacher said, "She is so eager to be baptized. Why are you trying to hinder her? The Lord will take care of all these other matters later on." So I was baptized, but for a year-and-a-half I didn't tell anyone, not even my parents.

Soon, my father began to make arrangements for my marriage and he brought many proposals. I did not dare tell him I was a Christian, but just keep on refusing all the proposals. One day he got very angry and said, "If you're not going to get married, I'm going to leave this house." If he left, there would be no one to take care of the family. I couldn't let that happen, so instead, I left and went to live with my Christian sister in another village.

We often prayed about my parents' intentions, for my father and brother-in-law continued to harass me about marriage. In the meantime, my sister and I went to a meeting where R.R.K. Murthy, an evangelist we had often heard on the radio, was speaking. When we shared the problem with him, he offered to speak to my parents, but they would not listen to him either. So Mr. Murthy told us about the Bible school in Shamshabad and suggested that I go there to study for six months.

Again, my parents were dead set against my wishes. They were angry enough that I had already disobeyed them regarding marriage, and now that I wanted to study somewhere far away, they simply could not accept it. I argued that it would be only for six months and Mr. Murthy would take the responsibility for getting me to school and then back home again. Finally, after a lot of discussion and many arguments, they agreed.

When I came to Bible school, I found out that the full program was three years. I immediately wrote my parents and told them that I wanted to stay for the full program. By this time they knew I was beginning to make my own decisions. What could they say?

Today I've come the point where my family no longer interferes in my personal spiritual life. Even when I go home I have Bible reading and prayer, and participate in Christian activities. I don't feel so much opposition any more, yet I am concerned about my family.

Although my parents know about Christ, they still feel that it would be too much of a burden for them to accept the Lord. I wish they could experience what I have experienced. When I was a Hindu, I had everything I needed materially, but I didn't have any real joy in my heart. When I became a Christian and came to Bible school, the fellowship and sharing among believers brought me real joy.

M. N. Jeevaratnam

To hear his story you must venture deep into the forest of teak and bamboo, where tigers and wild boar roam, and rope-like vines tangle themselves between the trees. For 48 years, Mennonite Brethren pastor M.N. Jeevaratnam has been working in tribal villages of the Amrabad plateau in the southeastern corner of the region where Mennonite Brethren missionaries have worked since before the turn of the century. Visitors are rare, and as you stoop to enter the tiny doorway of the house, you are greeted with bright garlands of oleanders and marigolds. The mud-brick house is filled with the spicy scent of mutton curry which Jeevaratnam's wife cooks over a smoky wood fire. After cool water is drawn to wash hands and feet, reed mats are rolled out on the floor and leaf plates are piled with generous handfuls of steaming rice.

Jeevaratnam and his wife have made their home among the Hindus and the Chensulu tribal people who live scattered in the Amrabad Hills. They feel a great burden for these people, for many of them have never heard of the way of Christ. Because of his age, Jeevaratnam now finds it difficult to travel into jungle areas to visit them. Yet he sees how receptive they are to Christianity. On a recent visit, some of the tribesmen asked, "Sir, don't you have a relative or an acqaintance that you could send to us?" They also said, "Perhaps there is someone who can teach our children."

"We pray for more people who will hear and obey God's

call to work among these people," says Jeevaratnam. He remembers how God taught him to obey, for he had not always worked in Amrabad willingly. In fact after his education he was glad when God led him to teach for four years in the school where he had earlier studied. Then one day the missionaries met with him to report that the elderly preacher working in Amrabad had died and there was no one to take his place. "Perhaps you should take up this work" they suggested.

Though he personally did not want to go, Jeevaratnam finally agreed in order to please the missionaries. But he was unhappy there and continually looked for excuses to come home. After one year he said to the missionaries, "My parents are very old and they need me. I must go back to my village." But they replied, "Once you put your hand to the plow, you should not look back." Dissatisfied with this advice, he looked for more reasons to leave.

But one day as he was alone in his house, Jeevaratnam had a type of vision. Suddenly he felt a gust of wind coming behind him. There was a big fire approaching him and he was afraid that it would burn him. In his fear, he began to sing a Telugu song which proclaims God's love. Then he felt someone's hand on his shoulder pushing him to sit down on the floor. When he looked around and saw no one, he concluded that the Lord was telling him to settle there. From that event, over 40 years ago, to the present day, Jeevaratnam has made Amrabad his home, and the work of building God's church there among villagers and tribal people his concern.

Finding enough pastors to take up the work has always been a problem for India's Mennonite Brethren church. With an estimated 28,000 Mennonite Brethren Christians scattered in about 750 villages, the preachers have to do much travelling. The 130-150 people on the "preacher's list" find that they can best minister to the villagers by working in circuits. As a circuit leader, Jeevaratnam pastors a central church and ministers to people in a cluster of neighboring villages as well.

Altogether he is responsible for 40 villages, where he and five other preachers conduct weddings, funerals and baptisms in addition to regular and special services. In some circuits, each preacher has up to 10 or 15 villages under his care. He may find it impossible at times to hold regular meetings in all of them.

Obeying God's call has not always been easy. Jeevaratnam has faced the problems that most Christians, and especially those in the ministry, face in India. For instance, he has to deal with the nominalism of many Christians who deny their faith because of government privileges which they qualify for as Indians of the "scheduled castes" (includes outcastes), but which they lose when they confess to be Christians. When these privileges are such things as free education for their children, priority in certain jobs, and other economic advantages, this temptation becomes a very serious one.

Despite government attempts to abolish the age-old system of caste divisions, even in the smallest Hindu villages the complex system of strict vertical relationships stubbornly remains. The outcastes which Mahatma Gandhi sympathetically renamed "Harijans" or "children of God" are still considered "untouchables" in many of the villages. How, then, can an outcaste Indian Christian dare to speak about his faith with those above him?

While many Indian preachers minister only among people of the lowest castes of Indian society, from which they themselves usually come, a few are bold enough to approach people of higher castes and to answer their questions. When a group of caste officials and medical doctors came to his village one day, Jeevaratnam visited them. When they asked him who he was, he replied, "I'm a Christian pastor." They just scoffed at him saying, "Your religion is not for us." But Jeevaratnam continued, "What would you think if a dog came in, and I saluted it and bowed down in front of it while you were standing here? Naturally you would be angry and say, 'This fellow is a fool. We are important doctors and educated men. Why is he respecting a dumb dog instead of us?" The men agreed that indeed they would become angry. So Jeevaratnam said, "This is how it will be some day. The Lord will be angry with you. You have ignored the Lord God who is almighty and the creator of all things. Instead you are bowing down to idols and creatures." Surprised by his confident speech and authoritative tone, the men allowed Jeevaratnam to speak.

Often a Christian pastor must take risks in the face of caste pressures. After Jeevaratnam shared about Christ to a group of caste people, one man from the prestigious Reddy caste believed and requested baptism. Jeevaratnam hesitated because he was concerned that the villagers would react with hostility to a high caste man joining in faith and baptism with outcastes. But this Reddy man was so adamant in his request that Jeevaratnam finally consented and baptized him with the others. He reports that this believer is continuing in his faith despite the strong family and community pressures upon him.

Jeevaratnam wins the respect of caste and outcaste people alike, partly through his role as teacher which he has always included as a major part of his ministry. He presently has about 25 students, one group during the day, and another in the evening. The children arrive carrying school books, slates and chalk, and sit down for class under the shade of a neem tree which grows beside the cow stable in Jeevaratnam's backyard. Besides reading and writing, he also takes the opportunity to teach the children Christian songs and Bible stories. In spite of the Christian emphasis, many caste people choose to send their children to him rather than to the government school in the area.

Christianity is also introduced by special events which attract the interest of the villagers. At Christmas hundreds of people attend programs in which the meaning of Christmas is shared. And when Christian films are shown, such as the movie in the Telegu language on the life of Christ Karunamayudu *(The Merciful One)*, thousands of people turn up.

As the leaf plates are cleared away and a cow is shooed from the open doorway, Jeevaratnam glances at the schoolchildren who are waiting in the backyard for their classes to begin. "There are so many opportunities to serve the Lord," he says. Jeevaratnam believes that Christians are called to obedience. Then God will do the rest.

Frieda Esau

zaire

ZAIRE

Population: 30 million
Capital: Kinshasa
Languages: French, Lingala, Swahili, Kikongo (and
               variant, Kituba) and Tshiluba
Religions: Roman Catholic (50%), Protestant (30%),
               African indigenous churches (16%),
               Animist, Muslim (Evangelicals: 17%)

Mennonite Brethren Conference of Zaire: 35,000 members, 300 churches and worship groups. Missions/Services ministries: Bible teaching, pastoral resource ministries, medicine, literature, vocational training, high school teaching.

Mennonite Brethren mission work in Zaire dates to 1912 when Aaron and Ernestina Janzen took up an assignment with the Mennonite agency, the Congo Inland Mission (now the Africa Inter-Mennonite Mission). In 1924 they began an independent work at Kafumba, which was officially accepted as an MB conference mission in 1943. By that time, other MB work had also taken root in the Bololo region northeast of Kafumba.

The proliferation of mission stations in the 1940s and 50s, together with the takeover of one of the fields of the Unevangelized Tribes Mission in 1953, helped the Mennonite Brethren church become established. The country's independence from Belgium in 1960, followed by a period of rebellion and persecution, only strengthened the emerging church as an indigenous body. It was officially incorporated as such in 1971, and assumed administrative responsibility for schools and other institutions begun by the mission. The church has continued to grow rapidly, with membership mushrooming from 12,000 in 1973 to almost 35,000 in 1984.

Djimbo Kubala

When an African speaks in a parable, its meaning is not always as straight-forward as a Western mind might like, but its truth has a way of striking home. So it is with a word-picture told by the most senior pastor in Zaire's Mennonite Brethren church today, Djimbo Kubala.

"If a blacksmith needs help to carry his anvil to the place where he wants to fashion a knife," Djimbo says, "he cannot claim ownership of the knife when it is finished. Part of it belongs to the one who helped carry the anvil."

It is his way of acknowledging the part North Americans have played in fashioning the Mennonite Brethren church in Zaire. His affirmation that the foreigners are joint "owners" of the church comes out of a long experience with them.

Tata (father) Djimbo, in his seventies and almost blind, is one of a few who have seen the church through its entire history. He was one of the first converts after the first missionaries set up a mission station in Kafumba in 1924. He was vice-president of the Mennonite Brethren conference when it took official shape in 1971. He is still present as the church struggles to become self-supporting and self-governing.

He still lives at Kafumba in a small but comfortable tin-roofed house. Just up the hill is a large church which dominates what is still called "the mission," perched on a slope overlooking some hills and a valley filled with lush tropical growth and palm forests. Other houses are occupied by Zairians employed at the primary school, secondary school and dispensary which the missionaries used to run. The site also includes skeletons of a former printshop and another school building, ransacked during the Mulele rebellions of 1963-64.

Since the rebellions, missionaries for the region have lived in the city of Kikwit, two hours to the north by four-wheel drive vehicle. Kafumba remains the headquarters for a ten-church district of the conference's northern region. And Djimbo remains as a respected patriarch of the community, preaching when he can, but not travelling among the churches as much as he used to.

Djimbo was the first African to be groomed for leadership in the Mennonite Brethren church. Born as a slave in the household of a tribal chief, he was sent to school at Kafumba shortly after Aaron and Ernestina Janzen had built the station. (They had served for some years earlier under the Congo Inland Mission in south-central Zaire.)

The Janzens adopted him, for his owners had virtually abandoned him. As he lived with the missionaries, and as they learned his language, he began to hear the "God-message" they had to tell. It was simple: God loved the world enough to give his only son to die for it—and for Djimbo himself.

"It was heavy in my heart that God would do this," he says. In the religion of his tribe, there was a concept of one supreme god, Mawesi, a vague being whose existence was prominent in the stories passed on orally through the generations. But no one knew what this god was like, or that people were responsible to live for him.

When Djimbo became a Christian in 1927, he knew he was going against the grain of other boys his age. Already, Catholic missionaries had made inroads in the region, he said, and had initiated a rumor that Protestant missionaries would take converts away from their families and transplant them somewhere far away. Even if that were true, it didn't bother Djimbo, since he and his family were rootless anyway.

There were immediate changes in his life—particularly in his way of talking and relating to people. He also became free from superstition, throwing away a charm he used to wear which was supposed to prevent rain during his trips with the chief.

After several years in the mission school, Djimbo himself was sent to teach at a school at nearby Kiandu. Meanwhile a church was coming into being at Kafumba, and it wasn't long before the missionaries asked him to return to the station, take further Bible training and become the first African pastor.

Since his ordination by Aaron Janzen in 1938, he has been the pastor at Kafumba, serving as a model for many other leaders who have lived and trained at Kafumba. In the early years he also helped in the monumental task of translating the New Testament into the Kituba trade language.

Djimbo Kubala takes particular pleasure in telling of the 1963-64 rebellions, which have become legendary in many church histories in Zaire. Missionaries had only recently returned from their exile imposed on them in 1960, when the country was jostling for independence from Belgian colonial rule. In the still shakey political scene, Pierre Mulele and followers tried to take control of the country, but were dubiously successful only in the western province of Kwilu.

Fleeing from the pressure of siding with the rebels or facing torture or death, most of the missionaries either returned home or retreated west to the capital, Kinshasa, to carry on the work through radio, translation and literature production.

Djimbo hid in the dense tropical rain forests in the Kafumba area. He was soon followed by other members of his flock, and for almost two years he and his family lived in crude temporary shelters of leaves and sticks. They risked malnutrition, feeding on whatever edible herbs and fruits they could find. Their clothes wore out. Djimbo says that another Mennonite Brethren pastor even had to order in some emergency clothes from Mennonite Central Committee before he could decently come out of hiding.

"God blessed us the most at that time," Djimbo reflectes. In the early mornings and late evenings, the believers would pray together. If they sang, it was very quietly, for one never knew if rebels or suspicious government soldiers were near-by. A personal sign of God's faithfulness during that time was that the beloved pastor was healed of headaches that had been bothering him before.

When rumors began circulating that the uprisings were over, how were Djimbo and his wife to know for sure if it was safe to come out of hiding? Civilians would sometimes come to the edge of the forest and call out that it was safe to come out. Suspicious of trickery, Djimbo would call back, "If you call a dog don't wave a stick!" and withdraw farther into the forest.

Finally, when the rains started, and Djimbo and his family failed to find adequate shelter, they took it to be the Spirit's leading them to come out of hiding. The believers were overjoyed when they saw their veteran leader alive.

Djimbo reflects that since that time, with the missionaries gone from Kafumba, the onus has been on him to see that more shepherds of God's flock emerge from the younger ranks in the area. It has been a gift which the church could hardly do without. "It has been a particular thrill for me to teach in the church, and to see others not only become Christians, but to go into the pastorate," he says.

He tells of one young man of Kafumba who had no respect for the church, living a life of thievery and adultery. Djimbo managed to gain his confidence enough to have Bible studies with him which eventually led to a commitment to Christ. "His conversion reminded me of Paul's," he said. "After persecuting the church, he turned around completely to serve it instead." That man is now serving as a pastor in

Kikwit.

"With God's help the church will grow to maturity," Djimbo sums up as he gratefully acknowledges the gifts of other men and women who now serve in his district. He adds, however, that from his perspective, the churches still appreciate and need the support of missionary teachers and church resource people.

His parable comes to mind. Missionaries helped carry the church during those early times, and they will remain today as enablers in the church. Djimbo is saying, in effect, "Let them continue to stand by us and share in the blessings of God as his church is fashioned on the anvil of time."

Byron Burkholder

Kasai and Balakashi Kapata

What do you talk about when you're buried up to your neck in the earth, surrounded by the handful of scruffy guerillas who put you there? When Kasai Kapata was in that position he spoke up with "Comrades, it's a good thing that I am here in this grave."

"They thought I was crazy to say that," he now remembers, twenty years later. "But they also knew I was a preacher in that area."

The story has become legend in the Mennonite Brethren church of Zaire. It was 1964, when the followers of Pierre Mulele still had much of the Bandundu region under their control. For over a year, they had been carrying on a campaign of rebel indoctrination in the region's villages. Many, especially Christians who resisted Mulele's anti-church philosophy, had gone into hiding in the dense forests. The rebels had destroyed Protestant and Catholic missions, including the Mennonite Brethren ones at Matende, Lusemvu and Kafumba. It was near Kafumba that Kasai was arrested.

What led up to those faith-testing three days was a story in itself. The son of a witchdoctor, Kasai had been educated at the Kafumba mission, and eventually became the young assistant of pastor Djimbo Kabala (now a patriarch in the national church) at the mission church.

Not long before the rebellions he had read in the sixth chapter of Isaiah, "Whom shall I send? And who will go for us?'' That passage had driven him to a new commitment to Christ and his service, even though he had been in evangelism and church work for almost eight years, both in the Kafumba area and in a village near Kikwit, 60 kilometers away.

When the rebels swept into the Kafumba area, the missionaries were forced to evacuate to the state-controlled city of Kikwit or the national capital Leopoldville (now Kinshasa). Djimbo also left soon, hiding in the forests near the station. Before long, Kasai and his family were among those making an exodus from Kafumba.

The first thing that made them put their faith on the line, however, was not a rebel attack, but a fluke of nature. Under cover of night, Kasai and his party came to the Kwilu River, which had to be ferried by canoe. As his wife Balakashi and their two children followed Kasai in a separate canoe, a strong current caught them and overturned the vessel.

Balakashi desperately held on to the youngest one and shouted for the other to hang onto the canoe until help came. The men, who had already landed, quickly saw what the problem was and paddled downstream to where the current had carried the canoe.

''I was sure that neither child would live, they had swallowed so much water,'' Balakashi recalls. ''But they did recover, and that convinced me that the Lord was there and would continue to be with us.''

They arrived at their home village near Gungu, only to find that the rebels were in control there too. Like many others of the common people, Kasai was forced to join them, even though they knew he had been a leader at the mission. (Some rebel leaders were not as radical as others, Kasai explains. Otherwise he might have died.)

His forced labor of supplying food for the rebel soldiers was not exactly enjoyable, he remembers. ''It was hard for me as a Christian to watch the beatings and killings which were going on, but I did have the opportunity to witness to the rebels and help foster peace among the villagers themselves." Sometimes it was difficult, because, as someone who had been associated with the mission, he was regarded with some suspicion.

Meanwhile, Balakashi and the children were constantly being challenged to keep trusting God, especially when Kasai's work called him away from home. On one of the occasions when the villagers had to evacuate to the bush because of fighting between the rebels and government soldiers, one of the children asked her, "How are we going to save ourselves?" Her quiet reply: "The Lord saved us at the river, and he will take care of us now."

After several months, Kasai felt compelled to return to Kafumba to retrieve some of the family's belongings and see how the believers there were faring. As he approached the station, he was stopped by a group of rebels, who recognized him as the former preacher. The most vocal ones in the group were anxious to see him dead and ordered him to begin digging a grave for himself with a hoe they had on hand. A few others pressed for mercy; at one time they had respected him as a Sunday school teacher and could not bear to see him killed. So the captive was buried up to his neck while the rebels decided what to do with him. One of the leaders offered to drive a truck over his head.

The three days Kasai spent in his own grave was a time of soul-searching, he recalls. "Would I persevere and stay with my calling to be a pastor? Or would this experience suddenly shatter the reality of God's clear voice just a couple of years ago?" The hate that surrounded him during those uncertain days also tested his love for his enemies. These former Sunday school pupils—how could they have turned against him? How could he love them?

As he thought and prayed, his commitment to God only strengthened, and his love only grew. His attitude even became cheerful, something with which his captors couldn't cope. Finally, at the urging of his former pupils, he was released and allowed to continue to the mission, which by now had been ransacked by the rebels.

Even though the area was still under the tenuous control of the rebels, Kasai was able to bring some of the believers together and meet with them until government troops regained control of the area, and used the mission as a base.

Then Kasai was arrested again—this time by the government authorities—for protesting the soldiers' intention of stripping the tin off the mission buildings. It took a special appeal to the mission's legal representative in Kikwit, John Kliewer, to get his release.

Kasai was instrumental in rebuilding the congregation after the anarchy and confusion of the Rebellion had faded. "When people came back (to church) they listened to and obeyed the Word when it was preached." To this day, Kafumbu remains among the most active districts in the Mennonite Brethren church, thanks largely to the continuous service of Kasai's mentor, Djimbo Kabala.

Only a few years after that time of persecution, however, a call came to Kasai from a small Protestant fellowship in Pai Kongila, west of Kafumba, where the Mennonite Brethren mission was on contract to provide staff for a large medical centre.

Kasai and Balakashi have been there ever since, serving in the strength of the God who saw them through the trials of the Rebellion. Through their avid evangelism in the Pai Kongila area, ten congregations and ten extension churches have sprung up, with a total membership of over 2,300. Five of the congregations recently formed their own district, Lukula II, with their own ordained pastor.

Asked whether they think the hardships have been good for them, Kasai says, "I have discovered that the Lord has cleansed us through these experiences." As he had told the rebels, "It's a good thing that I am here in this grave."

Would he go so far as to say that another rebellion would be good for the church? Kasai smiles as he says, "Yes, I believe so. Paul says that during a time of persecution, the church becomes stronger.''

He points out that even though Zaire's political climate is, at least on the surface, one of the most stable in Africa today, ''there is a persecution of sorts: the coming of the sects. It is getting serious, especially in the cities where they are reaching the business people and the influential people of the community.'' Even in Pai Kongila, Kasai says, ''the Jehovah's Witnesses are becoming stronger. It requires that we pray that those who are weak in the faith will remain strong.''

Byron Burkholder

Tshimika
and Makeka
Mutondo

In the region around Kajiji, southwestern Zaire, Tshimika Mutondo and his wife Makeka are known as pillars of the church. He is the much-loved senior pastor with the booming voice and no-nonsense preaching style. She is the woman who has dreams and teaches other women the Word of God. Their thatched roof stone house on the edge of the historic Kajiji mission is a place where many have found counsel, fellowship and warmth.

They both came to a living faith in Christ in the late 1930s when the Unevangelized Tribes Mission was still doing pioneer evangelism in the area. For Makeka, it was the question of creation that started her on the road to faith.

"Who made the heavens and the things around us?" she asked as a girl. None of the stories of the Chokwe tribe had any clear answers, and that bothered her. One night she wept over the question.

A glimmer of an answer came when pastor Manasseh from nearby Kingwangala came to her village and spoke about a Creator in heaven. But it wasn't until she and several other girls were chosen by the village chief and sent to the mission school at Shambungu (the forerunner to Kajiji) that her quest was finally fulfilled. And she heard much more than just the creation story; she heard about the Creator's great love which caused him to send his only son from heaven to die for her sins.

One night she had a dream in which she saw herself in a crowd of people. Those on the right disappeared, while on the left, only she and a fellow student remained. The dream reminded her of a sermon an African pastor had preached, that those who did good would go to heaven, while those who did evil would remain to face judgement. Cut in her conscience, she accepted the creator-God as her personal Lord, and was baptized in 1940.

Pastor Tshimika's testimony begins with the question of faith. He had heard a UTM missionary preach on John 3:16— "that whoever believes in him, will not perish, but have eternal life."

"I began to wonder what believing was," he recalls. When he asked the missionary he replied, "If you see something you want, you will go and get it, because you believe it is really there for the taking." The missionary told him that if he believed in the "God-message" and his offer of salvation, he would go to God's "village."

Tshimika made his commitment to Christ when the same missionary returned and spoke on the necessity to confess one's sins to God in order to receive His gift of forgiveness. Such a step was really believing. The faith of the Chokwes, Tshimika explains, included a concept of *Nzambi* (God) who was everywhere, but there was nothing specific in that belief. "We didn't know where Nzambi was," Makeka adds. "He was everyone's and nobody's God."

Almost immediately since they were married in the early 1940s, the two have been known as a pastoral team. Makeka had learned to read at the mission school and taught others from what she read in the Bible, and from the instruction she received from sermons on Sundays. When others expressed an interest in salvation, she took them to her husband or other leaders in the church for further instruction. She was even called "pastor" by some of her peers.

"It was really the Spirit of the Lord who was teaching us," says Tshimika, who himself never took formal Bible training, save for several two-month pastors' seminars led by the missionaries. His own call to the preaching ministry came shortly after the UTM work was turned over to Mennonite Brethren missions in 1953. Missionary Abe Esau asked Tshimika one day, "Why don't you follow the call of God and enter the pastorate?" Tshimika was afraid to commit himself to the responsibilities which came with a pastorate. Several months later, Arnold Prieb asked the same thing, and again he hung back.

Then it was Makeka who asked why he was hesitating. "Don't you remember the time when you were offered the mechanic's job, then the store-keeper's job, and they both proved to be God's will, though you had rejected them at first?"

Finally, one night, a person in white appeared to him in a dream and asked, "Why are you rejecting the call of God? Will you be like Jonah, who ran away from him?" The dream was the final catalyst which persuaded him to agree to become ordained as the first Zairian pastor for the Kajiji area since the coming of the Mennonite Brethren. His charge was to be resource person for all the churches in a region stretching several days' walk away.

That has been his calling since, though the churches have grown, the districts have multiplied, and more pastors have been ordained. Today he performs baptisms and communion for six congregations (and several extension points) without ordained pastors. When he visits a church, often traveling on foot, he stays for several days, conducting evening seminars on such topics as stewardship and the Christian family.

The Tshimikas' influence has been spread over a wide area, including some villages in Angola, which occasionally send people across the border for counseling. "People here have a great hunger for the Word of God," Tshimika says. "And people are turning to the Lord."

He tells of one new fellowship in the region which came into being after the conversion of the village chief eleven years ago. Today, that chief is influencing other chiefs in the area with the gospel.

Makeka gives another story from their experience which illustrates the way God has used them as a team. She was giving a Bible lesson in the maternity ward of the Kajiji hospital. The lesson happened to be on the story of the dedication of the child Samuel to the Lord.

A woman, who was known for involvement in witchcraft approached Makeka afterwards and related her story: "I recently gave birth to a child, and it soon got sick and died. My husband became very angry and said, 'Whoever is responsible for the child's death I will kill.' [In African culture, sickness is often attributed to the spell-casting of a malicious relative or friend.]

"That night I had a dream in which my child came back to life and appeared to me saying, 'I am now in the hands of Pastor Tshimika. Don't allow Father to carry out his plan.'

"When I told my husband, he didn't want to listen. 'But someone has killed my child,' he kept saying—until one night he saw the same dream."

That couple, says Makeka, have now become Christians and have gotten rid of their bitterness toward the imagined killer of their child.

Byron Burkholder

Benzembali
ma Dembia

The average jail sentence in Zaire would likely strike a Westerner as a comedy of errors. The story of Benzembali ma Dembia would, in any case. The former police chief spent 10 years behind bars, receiving several reductions in his sentence after appealing personally to the president—all for a charge that was never proved in a trial. The irony was that on release from prison, he was given a job as security supervisor at the presidential palace in Kinshasa.

But jail was also where Benzembali, now 64, found Christ again after a long period of backsliding. It was where he became such an avid witness to fellow prisoners that he was later to become one of the key evangelistic workers in the Kinshasa region of the Mennonite Brethren church.

Benzembali's first real encounter with Christ happened early in his life, in 1942, five years after he had joined the puppet army of the Belgian colonists. That year a Protestant missionary came to his camp near Leopaldville (now Kinshasa), and preached a gospel message based on Jesus' words, "Ask and you will receive. . ."

Somehow the words struck a responsive cord in the young soldier. At the outset of his time in the army he had had a painful confrontation with authorities of the Catholic church, to which he had belonged since childhood in Haut-Zaire, the northeastern part of the country. The religious leaders had given him a physical beating for abandoning a woman they thought should be his wife. Since that time he had been in a kind of spiritual limbo. "I knew that God was good, but that things were very bad for me in the Catholic church. So I didn't go anywhere; I didn't pray."

But the gospel he now heard gave him an opportunity to ask God for new life through Christ— and he did. "That day it was like fire of joy burning in my heart," he remembers. And his life changed. He stopped drinking palm wine, and shortly after his conversion he earned a promotion to a sergeant's position.

He left the army in 1947 for a post as police officer in his home town in Haut-Zaire. There, in the absence of the strong barracks church which had been such a source of spiritual strength, his faith suddenly ran aground. The temptations of his old life returned in force. He married two wives, took to drink again and joined in on the corruption that still characterizes the police in Zaire. "I was just like a pig who has just been washed and then goes back to his mud puddle." he says.

In 1960, in the wake of the country's independence from Belgium, Benzembali's superior used his expanded powers to put him in prison, possibly to pre-empt any designs Benzembali himself might have had on power. The charge, which Benzembali wasn't given a chance to refute, was that he had sold government guns to hunters and had pocketed the money.

From prison, he made a series of appeals to high ranking officials in the government. Some reprieve came when the country's new president Kasavubu personally intervened, transferring Benzembali across the country, back to Kinshasa, and reducing his 20-year sentence by five years. But before the case could be followed up further, the wobbly political scene of the early 1960s left Benzembali all but forgotten. Kasavubu was first temporarily, then permanently overthrown by President Mobutu.

Just before the rebellions of '63 and '64 thrust the country into chaos, Benzembali had a mysterious dream in which a man told him, "All your friends have died there in Haut-Zaire, but you are alive and safe here in Kinshasa." Shortly afterwards, when the rebellions swept the county, Kinshasa was one city that was relatively safe. Benzembali now says that if he had been left in prison in his home region, he would likely have been the victim of a purge of prisoners. That assurance of God's faithfulness and protection led to his "re-conversion" in 1963, and the start of an active life of Christian service.

He bought a Bible and studied it diligently, and he talked enthusiastically about his faith. Although formal Bible education didn't come until 1973 when he enrolled in the Emmaus Bible correspondence courses offered by the Mennonite Brethren church, his previous church exposure helped enable him to be an effective Christian example among the prisoners.

His spiritual homecoming was so profound, in fact, that a year after his turnaround he was elected coordinator for all the religious groups in the prison—Catholic, Protestant, and the indigenous sect, Kimbanguist. The job meant being a liaison between the prison and outside groups who came to serve the prisoners. Through the groups' officials, he would organize church services and special events. He held the post until his release in 1974, preaching occasionally, leading many to Christ, and currying the favor of the prisoners and even the prison authorities.

During that time, the Lord tested his faith through family circumstances. His second wife in Haut-Zaire remarried. His first wife had followed him to Kinshasa and had been in contact with him during his first few years in prison. Eventually she also gave up the commitment to him. Says Benzembali, "It was a difficult time; my family was just fading away." However, his commitment to his spiritual work in the prison only increased.

Benzembali is matter-of-fact about the job he was given immediately on his release from jail—that of security supervisor at the presidential palace. "The president wanted old soldiers, because they were not considered as much of a threat as the younger ones," he says. But it was in that role that "many, many" came to know Christ through the tracts he would hand out on the way to work, on the special bus for palace workers. His excellent work record also earned him the respect of his superiors, so that he could go on witnessing without harassment.

Benzembali owes his calling into full-time evangelistic work primarily to his introduction to Nduku Moboy-Ayavea shortly after his taking the palace job. Nduku, Mennonite Brethren chaplain at the large Kintambu hospital in Kinshasa, had heard about Benzembali's experience through one of the hospital's nurses, a neighbor of the ex-prisoner. Just the person to have as an assistant at the hospital! he thought.

Originally at their meeting, Benzembali had wanted to ask Nduku for advice about starting a church in his home region in Haut-Zaire. But as their acquaintance grew, the opportunity for hospital work won him over. He came to spend much of his spare time doing visitation at the hospital and helping to establish a special church on the hospital premises. The involvement became a full-time one in 1979, when he retired from the palace.

God had still bigger plans in store for Benzembali, who still dreamed of planting churches. In 1981 his sister asked him to move out to Mai Ndombe, 60 miles northeast of Kinshasa, to manage a farming operation she owned. It was an unlikely place for a person of Benzembali's character to move to. The village had for years been hostile to missionaries attempting to establish a Christian presence. The most influential people in the community were the   *fetisheurs,* those engaged in witchcraft. The nearest Christian church was a Salvation Army group six miles away.

All the same, when Benzembali moved to Mai Ndombe with his new wife, son and mother-in-law, the four began holding services as a family. "Soon I began calling young people to the services and taught them songs," he recalls. The services became so popular that Benzembali began holding them at the farm, where there was a larger meeting place. Strangely, the *fetisheurs* were not concerned about this grassroots movement — at least not enough to drive him away. He enjoys telling of the first person who turned to Christ. Mbwangu, now secretary of the Mai Ndombe church, had had a dream in which someone told him, "You are doubting that there is a town in heaven. Well, look over there." Mbwangu looked, and saw a shining city in his dream. The next morning he came to Benzembali, asking questions about the faith. "He had not known the gospel before," Benzembali says, "so right there, I was able to explain the way of salvation." Mbwangu was the first of a string of people in the village to come to Christ, many of whom brought fetishes (witchcraft images) to burn in public. When Benzembali wrote Nduku about what was happening, the Mennonite Brethren churches in Kinshasa started getting enthused about Mai Ndombe as their mission field. While many of the other city churches had gone ahead with some degree of foreign mission involvement, this one would be an entirely African project.

Delegations from the regional headquarters of the church in Kinshasa started to pay visits, to encourage the new believers. On the third visit, just a year after Benzembali's move there, 27 people were baptized in the Mai Ndombe river. Four months later, 25 more were baptized, some of whom were from Ndombe, a village seven miles upriver. Since that time a daughter congregation has taken root in Ndombe.

By the grace of God, this work has become a fitting capstone on the life of someone who has been through a good deal of injustice and personal failures. Benzembali ma Dembia remains as a recent example of how the transforming power of the gospel in one person's life can spill over into the lives of many, many others.

postscript: prison revisited. . .

Early in 1983, Benzembali's sister, a Jehovah's Witness, became concerned about the enormous popularity of her brother's religion. This concern resulted in bitter feelings between them. The outcome of that bitterness was another prison term for Benzembali, allegedly for negligence in the farm's management. "The real reason was that I was preaching in the villages," Benzembali says, "although there had been an error on one invoice, which provided a pretext for my arrest."

During his 60 days in prison, he continued to do what he knew best; he preached the gospel. The Church of Christ in Zaire, the umbrella organization for all Protestant churches in the country, even paid him to be the prison's religious advisor. His sister's charges were finally proved groundless, and since his release he has been back in Mai Ndombe, keeping the work going.

Byron Burkholder

paraguay

PARAGUAY

Population: 3.1 million
Capital: Asuncion
Languages: Spanish, Guarani
Religions: Roman Catholic (96%), (Evangelicals: 1.8%)

Mennonite Brethren conference of Paraguay: 1) Spanish-speaking Convention: 900 members in 28 churches and extension congregations; 2) German-speaking Association: 1200 members, 9 churches.
Missions/Services ministries: Bible institute teaching, pastoral resource ministries, evangelism/church planting.

The work of Mennonite Brethren missions in Paraguay has gone through a significant evolution since 1935, when North American MBs first supported a ministry of Mennonite settlers to the Chulupi and Lengua Indians of the Chaco region. Medical and evangelistic ministries were gradually assumed by the colonists themselves, while Missions/Services concentrated its work on the evangelization of Spanish and Guarni-speaking Paraguayans in and around Asuncion. Another priority was the training of church leaders — initially in German, but increasingly in Spanish as new indigenous churches were planted.

Since 1973, an important stimulus to the growth of the Spanish churches has been Thrust Evangelism, a program of evangelistic film, preaching and follow-up. Thrust, under the leadership of evangelist Albert Enns, has been largely responsible for the founding of at least 18 churches and worship groups in the Asuncion area and eastern Paraguay.

Ezequiel Villar

"Sometimes I feel ashamed and hurt when I think of my family," says 24-year-old Ezequiel Villar of Asuncion. "But I can give thanks to God for teaching me that families don't have to be like mine was. If it had not been for Jesus Christ, I don't know what would have happened to my life." Today, he is an aspiring evangelist in Paraguay's Mennonite Brethren convention.

Ezequiel believes there were clues at his birth that God had a special plan for his life. Originally, like most Paraguayans, his parents were Catholic by tradition but rarely attended church or took religion seriously. While his mother was pregnant with him, Ezequiel's parents became Christians through a Plymouth Brethren church in Puerto Rosario, their hometown in northern Paraguay.

Unfortunately, however, Ezequiel's father did not grow in his new faith. When the family moved to Asuncion, the senior Villar took to alcohol, setting relationships within the family on edge and mistreating his seven children.

"My mother suffered for the lives of us children," says Ezequiel. "She fought with dad constantly and suffered a lot to protect us."

The fighting, alcohol, and the low moral standards in his family made Ezequiel bitter. "Why do I have to live in this home?" he asked. "I feel I'm on a different planet—like I'm in the wrong place and don't belong here."

The Villars' poverty didn't help. As a boy, Ezequiel shined shoes and sold newspapers in the street for some extra family income. In his teens he worked in a factory half-days.

Although his parents shifted from one church to another, sometimes renewing their commitment, sometimes slipping back, they always insisted that their children attend Sunday school at the nearby San Isidro Mennonite Brethren Church. However, by the time he was 14, Ezequiel was bored with Sunday school and began trying to analyze his life and its meaning.

It was during this time of questioning, at a Pentecostal evangelistic meeting in an Asuncion plaza, that Ezequiel made a firm commitment. "I had learned in Sunday school how to be saved," says Ezequiel, "but I'd never felt it was necessary for me. At this campaign I realized I had to make my own decision."

At the time the San Isidro church was going through some traumatic difficulties. Conflict among some of the leading members had resulted in a decline in attendance, until there was practically no church left. A new pastor, Sixto Mencia, had been sent to try to pull the church together again, and was in the process of forming a closely knit group of young people.

There had been 40 or 50 young people in the church," says Ezequiel, "but they'd all quit coming because there was no one who took any interest in them. But Sixto started working with the five of us that were left. He was a great man of God, a true pastor. He was like a parent to me amidst the conflicts and fights in my home, and during my own doubts about the existence of God."

Ezequiel was elected youth leader and Sixto helped Ezequiel develop his leadership abilities, teaching him as much as he could about the church and how it worked.

"The first time in my life that I stood behind the pulpit," says Ezequiel, "I was leading a Wednesday evening Bible study and prayer meeting. There were 25 or 30 people there and I was so scared I couldn't remember a thing I said."

Ezequiel's young faith took a severe test when he was fulfilling his obligatory two years of military service. The moral life in the military was low, and filled with tensions and struggles. In defense, Ezequiel began memorizing Bible passages.

"I learned many of the Psalms and Proverbs, and all of Timothy and Titus by memory," he notes.

In his teens Ezequiel managed to finish sixth grade at Asuncion's Albert Schweitzer School, a large Mennonite Brethren elementary and high school which offers quality education to lower income families.

Then, in 1980, Ezequiel received a scholarship from the Mennonite Women's Group in Filadelfia, which enabled him to live and study at the Asuncion Bible Institute of the Mennonite Brethren church. The fulfillment of a dream he'd had since his conversion proved to be crucial in his development as a leader.

It was during his time at Bible school, at a Youth With a Mission student retreat in Argentina, that Ezequiel felt God call him to a life of Christian ministry. The call was bolstered in the summer of 1983, when he and veteran missionary evangelist Albert Enns attended Billy Graham's Congress for Itinerant Evangelists in Amsterdam.

At the moment the future holds many possibilities for Ezequiel. He may work with Enns on the Thrust Evangelism Team, or continue for some time in pastoral ministry, and there is always the possibility of further education. He currently serves as assistant pastor of a daughter congregation of the San Isidro Church. "I will go where God leads me," says Ezequiel. "But now I have dreams of being an evangelist. I have a private dream of preaching to a huge multitude of people."

With this world of possibilities that God is opening up, Ezequiel sometimes feels he's in a dream. As an expression of his gratitude, he wants to spread the good news of the new life to others in his country.   *Adrienne Wiebe*

Sepe Lhama

When Sepe Lhama was born in 1914, he and his family were nomads. They lived in temporary houses of straw and sticks. They hunted wild pigs, deer and birds, and gathered honey, fruits and edible roots for food. Shamans (medicine men) protected them from evil spirits. Today, as a senior leader in the 1,000 member Lengua Christian Church, Sepe Lhama lives in an adobe house on his farm where he grows crops of manioc, cotton and peanuts.

Sepe Lhama and other tribesmen of his generation have experienced more change during their lives than any other generation in the history of the Lengua Indians. For hundreds of years the Lenguas had scraped for a living in the harsh environment of the Chaco region of western Paraguay. The Chaco is a huge, flat wilderness of open stretches of grassland alternating with dense forests of thorn trees and cacti.

"My grandparents gave me the name Lanangvay which means 'invited,' " says Sepe Lhama. "When I was a few years old my mother gave birth to another son. But my mother didn't want this son and killed it immediately after it was born. I was angry with my mother, because I felt alone. So people gave me the name 'Sepe Lhama' which means 'Only Son.' "

At the time, many children were dying from convulsions and influenza, and smallpox was plaguing the adults. Not wanting to see children suffer, the Lengua women would use herbs to prevent pregnancies and to induce abortions. Sometimes they would kill the new-born baby by filling its mouth with sand and abandoning it before it was eight days old, when the soul was believed to enter the body.

The children who did survive saw incredible changes occur among their people as traders, missionaries and settlers moved into the Chaco.

"The first white man who came to us was an English missionary from Mochlagua," says Sepe Lhama, recalling his boyhood. "He was accompanied by an evangelist, Jacob Yamit, of the Lengua Sur (a group of Lenguas from another region of the Chaco). They told us the story of how God created the world and man. It was difficult to understand."

When Sepe Lhama was 13, the first European Mennonites immigrated to the Chaco to establish agricultural settlements. "The news came to us that a group of whites had arrived," recalls Sepe Lhama. "When our elders decided to go there to verify it, they saw that the newcomers were a different type of people; they spoke differently than the Paraguayans. They bought sweet potatoes and manioc from us and paid with cloth."

The event which more than any other hastened the invasion of Latin America society was the Chaco War of 1932-35. With the Bolivians and the Paraguayans each claiming the Chaco as national territory, the fighting went back and forth over the lands of the Indians. The soldiers bought food from the Indians. Some Indians acted as guides for the soldiers. Soldiers killed some Indians as spies and raped Indian women. To protect themselves, the Indians moved further and further away into the bush, away from the fighting.

The Paraguayans ultimately won the war, and most of the Chaco formally became a part of Paraguay. Lhama's family, along with many of the Indians, began to migrate towards the Mennonite colonies, looking for work.

Seeing the growing Indian population around the colonies,

the Mennonites began plans for a mission outreach at Yalva Sanga, a large plain south of the colonies. With the help of the Indians they began constructing the buildings for a church, schools and homes for the missionaries. They were also instrumental in settling the Indians in villages and teaching them how to farm.

Instead of doing construction work like many of the other Indians, Sepe Lhama became the language teacher for Gerhard Giesbrecht, one of the first Mennonite missionaries to the Lenguas. "I don't know why they called me," says the aged leader. "I was not a chief, not in any position of responsibility. But I think it was a miracle that I became his teacher."

Lhama could not speak any Spanish, so at first he and Giesbrecht communicated in sign language. Slowly he taught Giesbrecht to speak Lengua, (the first white person to do so, as far as the Mennonites know), while Giesbrecht taught him some Low German.

It was during his years with Giesbrecht that Sepe Lhama heard the story of Christ. He heard that people were bad and God would pardon their sin. But he did not think he was bad; he knew he did not get angry or kill anyone or commit any serious crimes.

"Then one day a heavy situation came into my life," he recalls; "a sinful thing happened. And I realized that I was bad." It was late at night but he rushed to Giesbrecht's house. "I want to tell you something," he told the missionary, "but we have to go away from here."

They ran through the grass in the dark for about a kilometre to a quebracho tree, the hardwood tree of the Chaco. For two hours Lhama told Giesbrecht about his life, explaining in the end that he wanted to confess his sins to God and receive his forgiveness. "I never knew how to pray before," he recalls, "but at that moment the Holy Spirit taught me how and I prayed to God."

Sepe Lhama's conversion was the first in the missionaries'

eleven years of work with the Lenguas. Shortly afterwards, six of Lhama's friends also became Christians.

The missionaries taught the new Christians for five years after their conversions to be sure they understood the significance of their decisions. Then on February 24, 1946, the first seven Christians of the Lengua tribe were baptized.

Lhama experienced many changes in his life. "Before, I had always felt alone, and afraid of evil spirits," he recalls, "but now I have Christ as my companion. I had even wanted to be a shaman and to do so had to eat many poisonous things to show my power. But I quit all this. I also quit smoking, drinking and adultery."

Even before his baptism Sepe Lhama had gone to preach in the scattered Lengua villages (formed only since the white man's coming). He did not have great knowledge of the Bible then, but he told the people his own story. After his baptism the missionaries urged him to continue this work as a pastor in the newly emerging Lengua church.

The calling was dramatically confirmed several years later, in 1955. Lhama was sleeping one night, when he heard someone call his name several times. His wife Katarina, also asleep, said she had not heard anything. He got up quickly and went outside, asking who was calling him. He heard nothing more, and took this as God's call to serve him.

Since then Lhama has taken many Bible courses and continues to study. Now he is the regional pastor of all the Lenguas who live in and around the community of Yalva Sanga. For a time he was president of the six Lengua churches.

In his ministry he stresses the need for Christians to be in daily communication with God, and have close fellowship with each other.

"God teaches me in dreams," says Sepe Lhama. Once he dreamt that he had to put out a fire. When he awoke, trying to understand the dream's meaning, the Holy Spirit told him that there was a misunderstanding among some of the people.

So in his sermon he clarified this particular problem for the people. Later he learned that there had been a disagreement which was about to erupt into bitter fighting.

"Our way of life today is much less difficult than before," says Sepe Lhama, summing up the great changes his people have experienced in his life. "We live in peace and can produce our own food. We have received much help. If we are sick, we have a place to look for cures. But the greatest help we have received is the Word of God that strengthens our lives and makes it possible for us to follow the right path."

Adrienne Wiebe

Fidelina Cuquejo

In 1915 when Fidelina Cuquejo was born, Paraguay was a poor, backward country with little contact with the rest of the world. World War 1 raging in Europe was of little concern to the families of Guarambare, the small farming village in eastern Paraguay where Fidelina grew up. As they had for generations, the villagers grew corn and sweet potatoes for themselves and sugar cane to sell for cash to the nearby sugar refinery. The Roman Catholic church, established when the first Europeans came to Paraguay 400 years earlier, was still the centre of the people's religious life, and they faithfully attended Mass every week.

Yet despite living in the same quiet village all her life, Fidelina was lonely. When she was in her mid-fifties her parents both died within a year of each other. Her husband of 23 years left her—childless, with only a young adopted boy to look after. Of her five brothers and sisters, only one sister still lived in Guarambare.

In 1972, the sister became very ill. While confined to bed, she took to reading the Bible for the first time in her life, and began to question some of the doctrines she had learned in the church. She became so affected by her reading, that when Fidelina brought the priest to hear her confession before she died, she refused to comply. Fidelina remembers her saying that she had learned that Christians should confess directly to God.

After her sister's death, Fidelina's loneliness grew. "I didn't want to go out of the house alone," says Fidelina. "People talked about me because I was old and alone. I couldn't sleep at nights."

In the early 1970s, for the first time in Paraguay, religious groups other than Catholic ones were allowed to hold public meetings. One of the groups to take advantage of this new freedom was the Mennonite Brethren churches of Paraguay, who in 1973 formed the Thrust Evangelism team to travel among the small farming villages around Asuncion, the capital city.

Evangelist Albert Enns and the team came to Guarambare the year after the program was launched. Of special attraction to this small isolated community were the nightly evangelistic films which were shown in the large circus tent the team used.

A cousin urged Fidelina to come, but she kept making excuses until the third night, when she finally went with another devout Catholic friend. The first thing the two women saw when they entered the tent was a table with books and literature. Fidelina asked team member Alfred Klassen what the books were. "The Word of God, which gives people spiritual food," Klassen told her.

Fidelina bought a book and left her address so that she could receive more information. After watching the film and listening to the sermon, Fidelina put up her hand to indicate that she wanted Jesus Christ as part of her life in the way the evangelist described it.

But, unsure about this decision after her lifelong attendance at the Catholic church, she and a friend went to see the superior priest in a nearby town. Fidelina wanted to ask him about what the Mennonite Brethren evangelistic team was teaching and her friend wanted to ask about some literature that some Mormon missionaries had given her.

When Fidelina's friend showed the priest the Mormon literature, he told her that it was from the devil, and that she should pay no attention to it.

But when Fidelina showed him the literature and the Bible she has received at the Thrust meetings and told him that through reading it she had felt a change of heart and felt stronger, the priest only affirmed her. She should go where she would find truth, he said.

Feeling more secure about her decision, Fidelina began attending the small Mennonite Brethren fellowship formed after the campaign—although she continued to attend Catholic Masses as well.

Soon the meetings were held at Fidelina's house. Without electricity in the village (until recently), they met by the light of kerosene lamps. Fidelina would make hot coffee for the group in winter, and juice when it was unbearably hot in the Paraguayan summer. Besides providing the meeting place for the group, Fidelina acted as treasurer.

About a year after her first contact with the Mennonites, Fidelina went to Asuncion for a special program in one of the older Mennonite Brethren churches. As she watched the large group of Christians gathered there sharing communion together, she realized that she wanted to be baptized and become a full member of this fellowship of Christians.

Her decision to take the step of baptism was beautifully confirmed by a special sign from God. Here is how it happened: Since the beginning of her new relationship with God, Fidelina had tried several times to quit her lifelong habit of smoking. Embarassed by her lack of success, she had only told one other Christian about her problem. This friend had told Fidelina that only the Lord's help would enable her to overcome this, and baptism would symbolize the loss of everything of her old self. Together the two women had prayed about it.

The night before her baptism, Fidelina could not sleep because of an extremely sore throat. When morning finally came her desire ever to have a cigarette again was completely gone, and her baptism was one of the most joyous experiences of her life.

All her life Fidelina has believed in God and tried to do what he wants her to, but she says that it has only been in the last 10 years that she has discovered the possibilities of his deep joy and peace. She adds, "I was always afraid of the future before; I felt I couldn't survive alone." Yet now, through reading the Bible and meeting with a group of committed Christians, Fidelina's fears about life have been replaced with God's strength.

Adrienne Wiebe

colombia

COLOMBIA

Population: 27 million
Capital: Bogota
Language: Spanish
Religions: Roman Catholic (97%) (Evangelicals 1.1%)

Mennonite Brethren Conference of Colombia: 1100 members in 23 churches

Missions/Services ministries: evangelism, church planting, Christian education, Bible institute teaching, pastoral resource ministries

Mennonite Brethren missionaries first came to Colombia in 1945 to reach the people of the jungle Chocó region. Congregations, schools and clinics were begun, sometimes experiencing fierce opposition from officials of the Roman Catholic church, at that time a formidable political institution. In the early 1960s church planting ministries were launched in Cali, which eventually became the center for church institutions: a Bible institute, a high school and a camp.

Today, more than half of the congregations of the Mennonite Brethren conference are in Cali and the surrounding Valle region. Since the 1970s, Missions/Services has also helped establish two congregations in Medellin and Bogota. These in turn have been added to the conference, which today is self-governing and self-propagating, though still dependent on Missions/Services funding for leadership training scholarships, evangelistic ministries and the Bible institute in Cali.

Victor and Lucila Mosquera

Victor Maria Mosquera stood on the dock at Bebedo, waiting for a boat called *Esperanza,* or Hope. He had decided to leave the jungles of the Chocó to go to Colombia's coast, where he hoped to find tailor work in the town of Buenaventura (literally, "good adventure").

"For some reason the boat was delayed more than usual," recalls Victor, "so I went farther downriver to Noanama. There I met an old friend, Daniel Murillo. He discouraged me from going on because he knew I was a tailor and that Noanama had no tailor. That same day he got me orders for ten pairs of pants."

When the *Esperanza* finally came, Victor had decided to stay. He found plenty of work in Noanama. He also encountered the Mennonite Brethren missionaries there. He liked what he heard from them, and today, 28 years later, Victor's quiet but consistent leadership makes him a mainstay of the Istmina M.B. Church.

Victor's parents were farmers. Like most of the other inhabitants of the dense tropical jungles of the Chocó, the Mosquera family are descendents of African slaves brought to South America in the 1500s to work gold mines for Spanish conquistadores. Freed in 1851, they remained in the Chocó, eking out a subsistence living by mining gold in small family mines and growing plantain and bananas to eat and sell.

After only one year of school, when he was 12, Victor was

largely self-educated, studying every book or newspaper he could find. Apart from reading, drinking, smoking and dancing were about the only diversions available from the back-breaking work and never-ending humidity of life in the Chocó.

Religion for the Mosqueras was more of a mechanical act than a meaningful part of life. Victor, like his parents and theirs before them, followed the Catholic tradition inherited from Spanish mine owners.

"My father was an *alferez* (church official), and carried the statue of his patron saint in processions," he explains, "but my mother was not particularly devout. I never imagined there was anything else."

Victor took up tailoring after his father died. He married Lucila Aragon at 27, and shortly after his mother died two years later, moved off the farm to a larger town, hoping to find work at a garment factory. Unable to pass their medical examination he struggled along on his own for several years, then made his decision to seek a better life in Buenaventura.

However, eight months later when he returned to get his wife and son, it was not from Buenaventura, but from Noanama. And not only did he have a new job, he had a new faith. Victor had become acquainted with missionaries David and Daniel Wirsche through a friend who had already joined the Mennonite Brethren church. He read the books the missionaries loaned him, and attended Bible studies and services.

"They were different from Catholic services, which were still in Latin then," Victor says. "I liked what I heard, and I decided to accept the Lord."

When Lucila heard about Victor's new faith, she says, she "rejoiced with him." After the family's move to Noanama she began attending services with Victor and eventually decided to join the M.B. church also.

Victor became an active member of the church, and continued to find plenty of work in the village. Other Christians, however, were experiencing much economic difficulty, and persecution of evangelicals by Catholics was strong at that time in Colombia. Victor and Lucila, along with other evangelical Christians, sent their two sons away to a school the missionaries had opened for M.B. children. Persecution against them in the government-run Catholic schools was simply that intense.

Eventually most of the church members migrated from Noanama, and out of concern for his family and his sons' education, Victor also decided to move. He chose to settle in Istmina, a larger Chocoan town, because of the large Mennonite Brethren church located there.

That church was going strong at the time, with active youth and women's groups, a strong Sunday School program and a Colombian pastor. Victor liked to teach and was asked to take over the adult class. Lucila became a faithful participant in the women's society.

Tailor work was harder to come by in Istmina though, and living costs were higher. The everyday struggle turned into a crisis when Victor developed tuberculosis and had to spend five months recovering in a sanitorium.

"I really don't know how we made it," he remembers. "Business came to a standstill. The church and some individual brethren helped out, and Lucila did housework. I can't explain it, but somehow the Lord saw us through."

When Victor returned home he was able to complete construction on the house he and Lucila had begun earlier, "with the help of friends and the Lord." Victor was able to renew business with some of his past clients, and Lucila supplemented the income by doing housework and selling homemade candies and baked goods.

The economic situation for people in the Chocó steadily worsened, however, and life continues to be an everyday struggle. Victor and Lucila's sons, like many of the young people from the area, have moved away to seek better educational and employment prospects.

Through the tough times they have never forgotten their earlier source of help. "Just before I go out to sell the things I bake," says Lucila, "I pray that I'll be able to get rid of everything quickly so I can return home, to look after our two grandchildren. Invariably, God answers." (The children live with them because of a break-up in one of their own children's families.)

Victor, too, sees God's hand in everyday life. "The money that my daughter-in-law sends for the care of the children often comes late," he explains. One morning we had nothing to eat in the house. "I awoke early and prayed that the Lord would supply our need as he promised, so that no one would suffer. Before the grandchildren went to school Lucila found an egg the hens had laid, so they had breakfast. Later I went downtown to see if I could come up with anything. Sure enough, on the way I encountered a woman who owed me 800 pesos and wanted to pay me immediately."

Christianity has not necessarily made Victor and Lucila's circumstances easier. They are experiencing the same hardships as their non-evangelical neighbors. But they have something that keeps them going. They have found Hope.

Cheryl Martin

Carlos Romero

Carlos Romero's life is like the material he sells—not a rich extravagant brocade perhaps, but something more than gingham. "I believe if we put things in the hands of God," he says, "he will arrange them." The interweaving of events in his life show how this belief translates into experience

Carlos, the 62-year-old owner of a respected fabric business in the Cali suburb of Yumbo, was born into a poor family in rural Colombia. Abandoned by his mother at an early age, he raised and educated himself in his godfather's house. He started out selling material at age six, but soon picked up other odd jobs—shepherding cattle, shoe-making and carpentry. His struggle was always to find room and board in the cities where he worked; one time he spent three nights sleeping in a police station.

When he reached age 20, Carlos suddenly felt the impact of his solitary life. He yearned to know his mother and family. Although he had grown up Catholic and knew only the Lord's Prayer, he decided to pray that he would find his mother. He also prayed that he would find only brothers, for he could not bear the thought of discovering sisters who would likely have fallen into the same misfortune and prostitution as other girls from poor families.

One day Carlos found a note slipped underneath the door of his apartment—an answer to an ad he had put in the paper in hopes of finding his family. His family was living near

Bogota, the capital of Colombia. Quickly, the young man arranged a trip to Bogota. When he arrived, the first question he asked his mother as he stepped in the door was, "Do I have brothers and sisters?"

"Five brothers," his mother answered, "but no sisters." Carlos breathed a simple thanks to God. A strong thread was woven—one he would never forget.

The next years were ones of economic struggle for Carlos. He helped his new-found family set up a hardware business in Cali, but their mismanagement of money and his frequent dancing sprees caused eventual bankruptcy. When he heard of good business prospects in the Chocó jungles, Carlos and his new wife decided to set up shop in Istmina, a bustling commercial center in the Chocó.

The day his new hardware and fabric shop was opened, many curious customers crossed the threshold, including missionary John Dyck (who died in a plane crash in 1957). Dyck invited the young businessman to a series of evangelistic meetings in town. The first night, Carlos was so drawn by the message that he listened with full attention and made a commitment to Christ.

The next Sunday, as usual, Carlos and his wife worked in their store in the morning and went on an outing with friends in the afternoon. When the couple returned in the evening, they found they had been robbed of all the money they had made in the morning. "My wife said this was punishment from God," Carlos relates. "We decided then to close the store on Sundays so we could go to church."

The first Sunday they closed the store, people kept begging them to open it—but they went to church instead. The next day, Carlos sold all morning, afternoon and late in the evening. When he counted up the money, he found he had sold more that day than in two or three normal days of business. "We felt that was an answer from the Lord for our obedience not to sell on Sundays," Carlos says. Another tight thread was woven.

But a real plaid of events was yet to come during the height of "The Years of Violence," the decade of political upheaval from 1952-62.

His store business continued to grow in Istmina, and his good prices attracted some regular customers, including some Catholic priests and nuns. Since Carlos was known for his common sense and education, the priests would often come to ask his advice on correspondence they were sending out. One day a priest came to Carlos with a letter he had just written. Carlos began reading it aloud. When he realized he was reading a petition to the president to throw out all of the evangelicals of Istmina, he stopped abruptly.

"Look," he said, "you complain about the Protestants attracting so many followers. But why do you want to throw them out? Their dispensary is doing a good service in Istmina. They are helping the sick and giving good advice to the people."

"I tell you what," he continued. "You have a big house. You can put up a dispensary that's even bigger than the evangelicals'. But you don't need to throw the Protestants out."

The priest looked at him with disdain. "I see—you are Protestant," he said, as if he wished to spit on the last word.

"Well, if being Protestant means loving and doing good for the people, then yes I am," Carlos replied. The priest turned and stalked off. But a few days later Carlos was surprised to see the priest buying goods in his store again as if nothing had happened.

Although the priest never sent the letter, word came from the government one Easter week that all evangelical churches were to be closed. Carlos' church decided to carry all the benches from the sanctuary to the second floor of a member's house. "That Sunday the room was filled with more people than we'd ever had in church," Carlos remembers. Three nights later the police came and closed the place.

For the next couple of months the church held Sunday

school in different homes each week. Carlos gave much thought to the situation and one day made an announcement to the church. "I am asking you all to stand by me," he said. "I know of a place in Istmina called Pueblo Nuevo where there is a roof and a floor but no walls. We can meet there. We can even put up one wall to protect the person preaching. But we must all agree that if the police come and take one of us, then we all go to prison. We are together in this."

The church agreed with his condition and regular services were started once again. "The police often came and stood at a distance," Carlos says, "but we were never once molested."

After several months, the political situation eased and the evangelicals were allowed to return to their church buildings. Carlos' church even began a school. But one day Carlos heard that the mayor was closing down the school. He was confused —only a short time ago he and other church leaders had gone to Quibdo, the capital of the Chocó, to talk to the governor about the school. The governor had assured the men that there would be no opposition.

Carlos went to see the mayor. He found out, upon questioning the man, that the governor had not ordered the closing of the school but had merely asked how many non-evangelical children were attending. Carlos sent a telegram answering the question. That night at prayer meeting, Carlos received a reply from the governor: "Tell your teachers to continue the school." A few days later, Carlos found out that the mayor was expelled and another one was being sent in his place. "That was the end of any major persecution for evangelicals in Istmina," Carlos says.

Carlos' business continued to grow, and he made periodic trips to Medellin, the second largest city in Colombia. One day he took his oldest daughter, who was seriously ill, to the city for medical treatment. Then, instead of returning home, he decided to spend some time in another village in the Chocó; he simply wanted a change to unwind from his worries and responsibilities. But one night when he returned to his hotel room, he received a message to hurry back to Medellin. His daughter was on the verge of death.

"When I heard the news, I fell to my knees by the hotel bed," Carlos says. "I pled with the Lord not to take my daughter's life. I told him, 'If you need to take a life, take mine.' I struggled with God and with my sin long into the night. I didn't quit praying until I felt he'd answered my prayer. I told God right then, 'Thank you that she is alive.' I felt calm and reassured."

When Carlos arrived at Medellin, he was met by a distraught doctor and his friend. "Don't ever leave us another child like this," they told him. "Last night your daughter stopped breathing. We pronounced her dead. But we were frantic. We told your mother who was here crying, 'You believe in God. You pray.' Then we filled a tub of water and bathed the girl with wet sheets. Suddenly, she opened her eyes."

"What time was that?" Carlos asked.

"In the middle of the night. Somewhere around 3:00 a.m." Carlos was quiet. It was the time he had felt a peace in the hotel room the night before.

Seeing the way God pulled together the various threads in his life in the Choco motivated Carlos to take several weeks off work to travel around with a church lay leader in the region. Taking only enough merchandise to sell for daily expenses, he and the other brother shared the gospel in a large number of villages along the Chocoan rivers.

In 1962, Carlos and his family left the Chocó. He set up another shop in the mountain area of La Cumbre, where his six children attended the Mennonite Brethren school, Colegio Los Andes. When his children were growing up in the Choco, Carlos had prayed to God, asking that his children wouldn't have to suffer as rough a childhood as he had had, and that above all, they would receive the solid education he had missed. Now, years later, his petitions were being realized.

Not long after his children were in high school, however,

Carlos' store was burnt to the ground. Surveying the ashes of the former merchandise, Carlos' second son Jairo began to cry, for he was sure now he would never receive his education. "Don't worry," his father told him. "God is faithful." Carlos went immediately to the factories. Since his record was good, he received merchandise on credit and was able to set up another store in the town of Yumbo, outside Cali—a store which is still operating now, some fifteen years later. "The Lord took away everything," Carlos says, "Yet, he has given so much back."

One thing Carlos feels was a gift from the Lord recently, is a special trip to Israel. "In Istmina, when I accepted Christ, someone gave me a Testament which I still have," he says, holding out a small reddish book. "When I began looking through the testament I saw a picture of Jerusalem. I asked the Lord then to give me the opportunity to visit the Holy Land. At age 62, through Campus Crusade for Christ, I was given the chance."

When Carlos returned from Israel, he found another prayer had been answered; one-half of his business had been sold. He had asked God to help him sell a section of his store so he could spend more time working in the Yumbo Mennonite Brethren Church. He has always been active in the church—at one time serving as president of the church council—but now he would have more time to devote to his responsibilities as elder and song-leader.

Naturally, Carlos' life has not been unflawed. Yet, it is like many bright threads coming together—a workmanship of the One in whom Carlos so simply and continuously believes.

Frances Martens

Lucia Quiroga

The room was quiet and cool. Nothing moved except for the occasionally flickering flame of a candle on one end of a table. Across from it lay a mound of dirt. At the other end of the table was a container of water, across from that an incense-burner. Lying in the middle of the four elements of Fire, Earth, Water and Air was a Bible.

Lucia Quiroga entered the sanctuary soundlessly. She knelt on the floor and began the demanding physical exercises of Yoga. Soon the sound of her breathing was all she could hear. She closed her eyes and began to meditate, but her mind wouldn't focus. Suddenly an overwhelming feeling of emptiness and doubt swept over her. Her hands and arms froze in mid-exercise. A sound broke through the stillness—her own anguished voice.

"Why am I doing this?" she whispered. "God, where are you? Why can't I find you? Why are you hiding? I've been looking for you for 40 years. I've been travelling on the road to you; why can't I get to you?"

A bitter sadness rose in her throat and she tasted the salt of her tears. Her eyes glanced over at the elements and alighted on the Bible. Books had always been her source of comfort. She reached out for this one, opened it and read: "I will instruct you and teach you the way you should go; I will counsel you with my eye upon you."

Lucia felt a sudden flow of energy. She shouted aloud and

shut the book in her excitement. "Lord, then you do speak! You do answer. I'm going to stand on this answer."

Lucia's experience in the Yoga room came in the midst of a difficult quest that had begun in her childhood. Although she had been born into a Catholic home in Pijao, Colombia and educated by nuns in a private convent, she had never been a devout follower of Catholicism. Even later in her life when she became a primary teacher and had to teach the Catholic faith, she did so with a critical mind. "I got to know the Catholic religion inside and out because I was zealous to teach it properly," she says. "But there was nothing there that attracted me. It was such a hard religion of works, purgatory, heaven and hell. I learned to know the historic Christ but nothing of his love and promises."

What did attract Lucia and command her respect was something else—the spiritist sect of Rosicrucianism. Through her boyfriend's influence Lucia became fascinated with the sect, which taught people to overcome their environment through strict moralism, meditation and self-discipline. She taught herself everything she could find on Rosicrucianism.

"The power of the leaders impressed me most," Lucia says. "Once when I was 25 I was ill with tonsillitis. I went to a special ritual at 11:00 at night and came out completely healed."

During this time, however, Lucia began to have home problems that left her little opportunity to develop her occultic interests. After only 20 days of marriage she found out that her Catholic husband was a bigamist. Her father legally denounced and jailed the man and brought Lucia home to live. Since her father was a poor country blacksmith and she a schoolmarm, it became a constant struggle for her to bring up her young son, Edwardo.

In the political turmoil between the Liberals and Conservatives in the early '50s, Lucia moved to the city of Cali and found a job as a secretary. "At this time I tried to influence Edwardo with my philosophy of life in the occult," she says "but he refused to let me teach him. He was a nominal Catholic, so I let him be."

However, her son's lack of interest in no way curtailed her own avid desire to deepen her experience in Spiritism. Lucia explains that the "disciples" of Rosicrucianism tend to move on to specialize in different schools of thought, such as Theosophism or Gnosticism. She chose to specialize in the Universal School of Thought which emphasized astrology and Yoga.

Astrology fascinated her so much that she bought books and built up a large library on the subject. She developed expertise in writing horoscopes, and many would come to her for advice—especially the poor with whom she preferred to work. In Cali she became well-known as someone who could make predictions with surprising accuracy.

Yoga also captured Lucia's energies. "In Yoga you think of God and the transcendent. You aspire to become. You are always searching for something better—the Good, the Infinite."

Lucia not only practiced Yoga but taught others the exercises. Every day at noon she ran out of the office to the Yoga center to warm up before starting the class. It was during one of these quiet times, alone in the sanctuary, that God spoke to her in her anguished cry of doubt.

"I felt happy and euphoric afterwards," Lucia says, "I went back to the office and told two of my friends about it. One told me, 'Girl, you're crazy, the roof tiles are slipping from your mind.'"

Eight days later, the incident in the Yoga room was no longer so fresh in Lucia's mind. However, she had lost all desire to continue in Yoga, and resigned as a leader. When her class members asked about the sudden change she replied, "I'm confused. Let me alone. I'll find myself."

In the meantime, one of Lucia's friends invited her to an "interesting meeting." At first Lucia rejected the offer, but after she heard it had "nothing to do with spiritism and raising tables, "her curiosity was fanned, and she went.

When Lucia realized the meeting was a prayer group of Alpha-Omega Campus Crusade, her first thought was to get up and leave. However, she enjoyed the music and the words of the songs; and when the leader asked to talk to her personally, she consented.

During the conversation the woman asked Lucia if she had accepted the Lord. Lucia was confused. Of course, she had often accepted the Lord's Supper in the Catholic Church. No, the woman explained, had she accepted Christ as Lord and Savior?

Lucia became furious. "What is all this talk about Savior and Redeemer? There is no such thing as a Redeemer. There is only one way to be saved—you have to do it yourself." The leader didn't argue, but read from her Bible, "Behold, I stand at the door and knock. . . ." Lucia was silent. Then she said in a still voice, "Young lady, there isn't a person in the world that I wouldn't let in at my door if they wanted in. If the Lord is knocking on my life—let him in."

On the way home from the meeting, a confusion began in her head—one that became more intense by the moment. "What did I do?" she said out loud. "What's life anyway? Is it self-realization and arriving by one's own efforts? Or is it redemption—something that happens to you?"

She walked into her house and looked at her shelves full of books on the occult. These books symbolized many years of seeking. Lucia vacillated in her mind. Jesus she had known all her life—surely he was greater than books. But she had worked and lived with books all her life—surely they were more real and satisfying.

But Lucia remained confused. One day she quit her horoscope services. She told one of her customers, "I'm not sure anymore what is the truth. But if this isn't the truth, I can't mess with it." The customer recommended that she see missionary John Savoia, then pastor of a nearby church fellowship.

Lucia went to a Bible study at the Savoia home and found the group studying Acts 19:19—a verse about Ephesian believers burning books on witchcraft. Lucia was dismayed, and asked the group, "What kind of cave dwellers were these people here in the Bible? To burn books! Books are the source of wisdom and knowledge. What sort of superstition was that?" She also asked questions about the occult and why astrology was sinful. But when she was pointed to the Bible she scoffed and left very upset.

But the conflict continued to rage in Lucia for the next four months, causing a nervous reaction and fever. Doctors recommended psychological help. But one of Lucia's sisters called her son Edwardo who meanwhile had become a Christian through a colleague in Bogota.

Edwardo came to Cali immediately. He was shocked at how thin and sad his mother had become. "I'm going crazy," Lucia told him. "I've got to find the truth." Edwardo said he could do something for her. He had a friend Bernardo who had experienced the same things she had. "He speaks your language, mother," he said. "He came out of the occult and became a Christian. He was even a Mason—farther into it than you were."

A week later Lucia's fever cleared and she flew to Bogota, where she spent a long evening speaking with Bernardo, who had fasted and prayed to prepare for her visit. "That night I understood a man talking wisdom," Lucia says. "For every argument I had, he had the spiritual wisdom to answer from the Bible. I still remember his words, 'Astrology might guide the fool, but not the wise. The stars may be able to talk, but they can't determine the course of life. Only God can.' I knew then that the road is with Jesus Christ; every other road is false."

Lucia returned to Cali, peaceful and relaxed. Only one problem remained—what to do with all her erroneous books? She couldn't give them away, but neither could she find it within herself to destroy them.

Meanwhile, she was looking for Christian books to replace her other ones. A friend gave her one in which she read how Abraham did not even deny the Lord his only son. Suddenly, Lucia felt foolish for refusing to sacrifice her own books. "Lord, they're yours," she said. "Let them turn to ashes."

That Saturday, Lucia burned away the vestiges of her old life in front of a group of Christians who had gathered to praise and to pray. A woman at the book-burning was impressed with Lucia and invited her to a Presbyterian women's retreat.

At the meetings, the leader talked of "insignificant" sins. "Suddenly, the Holy Spirit confronted me with all the sins in my life," Lucia recalls. "I was upset. I told the leader, 'This Christian life is such a narrow road. I'll never be able to fit on it. What am I going to do now? I can't go back. I've burned all my other books."

The leader replied that she was right—that she couldn't make it on her own but only with the hand of Christ.

"In front of this woman, I really broke down and repented," Lucia says. "Up until then I hadn't considered myself a sinner. I simply thought I had been on the wrong road. Anyway, the woman prayed for me and gave a special bold prayer that the Lord would break the hold of Spiritism on me and that in four days I would be totally liberated. And I was."

Lucia was even more amazed that in three months the arthritis she had acquired during her years in the occult had completely healed.

Today she is a member of Cali's Bethel Church (Mennonite Brethren associated), teaching a juniors' class and serving as secretary. She is building up a Christian library and studying Greek. She is also considering the adoption of an orphaned child whose family was killed in a nearby earthquake.

Her influence on her family is significant—almost all her family have become Christians, including two sisters who had also been involved in Spiritism, and her elderly mother. Lucia energetically shares her testimony with the many guests who constantly fill her living room. "It seems that everyone who comes here to visit becomes a Christian," she says, laughing. Lucia's testimony is so vital because after years of searching and pain, she knows how dangerous the powers outside of Christ are.

"My experience now is beautiful and very different," she says, "I now sense the real presence of Christ and his love. Before I would constantly search in the heavens and call on God. Now I don't ask where God is. I know. He's with me."

Frances Martens

brazil

BRAZIL

Population: 125 million
Capital: Brazilia
Language: Portuguese
Religions: Roman Catholic (88%), spiritist, Protestant
              (9%). (Evangelicals: 8%)

Mennonite Brethren conferences of Brazil: 1) Portuguese-speaking Convention: 150 members, 24 churches, numerous "preaching points." 2) German-speaking Association: 1,600 members, 13 churches.
Missions/Services ministries: church planting, Bible institute teaching.

Mennonite Brethren in Brazil have their roots in the Mennonite immigration from Europe and the Soviet Union during the 1930s. Soon after their arrival the newcomers began reaching out to their Brazilian neighbors, and churches were established in the 1950s. In 1945, North American Mennonite Brethren missionaries entered Brazil to help with these ventures, beginning with an orphange ministry (which closed in 1966) and extending to church planting in the states of Parana, Santa Catarina, Rio Grande Do Sul, and Sao Paulo and Mato Grosso.

The Portuguese-speaking churches formed their own conference in 1966, though they remainded (and still do) dependent on North American subsides for evangelistic work and some pastoral support. Six years later, they merged their own Bible school with that of the German-speaking churches. The Bible Institute and Seminary in Curitiba remains the key institution for both groups, with an enrolment of about 100.

The German-speaking Association is largely independent of Missions/Services, but does draw on missionary help for church planting among Brazilians of German background. These ventures are particularly active in the state of Santa Catarina, where people have been reached through gospel radio and evangelistic thrusts.

94

Rita Rodrigues

Rita Rodrigues do Rosario spent 10 years of her childhood in Lar das Criancas (Children's Home), an orphanage in Curitiba, Brazil, begun by Mennonite Brethren missionaries. In October 1981 she returned to Brazil from a two-year Mennonite Central Committee assignment in Montreal, Quebec.

At the children's home, Rita says, she learned that all people are equal; in Montreal she realized that there were other people in the world besides Brazilians, that she was part of a larger, global community.

Here is the story of how God used Mennonites to work in Rita's life as told to Cheryl Martin:

I was born into a Catholic home in 1954, near Curitiba. When I was only two, my mother's conversion to a Pentecostal faith led to my parents' separation.

My mother came to live in Curitiba with her parents. Since she had to work days, my brother and I were sent to the Lars das Criancas, where we lived until I was 13.

Those were important years of my life. I learned that no matter who I am, I'm equal to everyone else. There were 70 of us children then—40 toward the end—but we were treated as equals.

When the home closed in 1966, we went to live with my mother again, and I attended a private Catholic school. I hit bottom there. I had grown up thinking Mennonites were the only ones going to heaven—and suddenly, I was studying in a Catholic school and living with a Pentecostal mother who didn't care to go to a Mennonite church.

In the Catholic school I tried to tell everyone about Jesus Christ, and they didn't like it. My background in the home helped in the religion class because I was the only one that knew where to find things in the Bible. But the teacher didn't like my answers, so he finally told me I couldn't come to class anymore. When we had Mass every Tuesday I had to sit at the back beside the director so that other kids would not follow my example of not making the rights signs.

After my graduation in 1969 I went to a teacher training school for three years, and then started working at a state bank.

Since I had moved back with my mother I hadn't been going to church. My brother and I prayed and read the Bible, but my mother wouldn't let us go to the Mennonite church unless we also went to her church, and we didn't want to. One Saturday night I was babysitting for a neighbor and the doorbell rang. Outside were two kids and Mr. Erven Thiesen, the former director at the home who had some connection with my neighbor. They told me about the Center (Mennonite Brethren) Church nearby. I went the next morning, and continued going.

After I had been there for two years I asked myself, "Am I Christian or not?" I realized that I knew a lot of Bible verses, and knew all the songs they sang. I had raised my hand many times during the evangelistic meetings at the home, but didn't know if one of them was valid. I talked to the Center Church pastor, and he gave me a series of Bible verses to study on my own.

I thought I wouldn't have any emotions because I was so used to doing these religious duties. But as I studied the verses they became very meaningful to me. One that has been with me ever since is Psalm 37:5: "Give your way to the Lord, trust in him, and he will do the rest."

I decided to get baptized two months later. I had never wanted to before because it meant working in the church. I knew I needed to make Jesus Lord of my life, day and night. With that came the decision to live not for money, but for others, and I changed my attitude about working in the church.

Then some dark clouds came over my life. That was 1975 and I was 19. After much dreaming, thinking and talking to my mother, I decided to look for my father. I couldn't remember anything about him, but my brother and I persuaded our mom to take action and find him.

She found his address, and I wrote, telling him I was his daughter and asking him to come visit us. I was anxious, though, because I was afraid it would change my life plans; I had already applied and been accepted for MCC's trainee program in North America.

It was my father's brother, however, who came to Curitiba to check if it were all true. My father was in the hospital, and my uncle didn't want to tell him if it were the wrong person writing. When he saw that we were his family he invited us to go to São Paulo, where they lived.

About a month later my brother and I went, on the Brazilian national holidays, September 7-9. I was really scared, and wanted to turn back, but my brother wanted to keep on going. We went to my uncle's house and my father was waiting for us.

I was very, very cold to him. I was surprised at my own reaction, but didn't want to let him know my feelings. But the next morning, as we were having breakfast, he began to feel really bad, and had heart pains. I thought, "Oh, he's going to die and not know my feelings."

His brother came and gave him a massage. When he was better we talked for a long time. My father gave us his side of the story, and it went along with what my mother said. I was very happy, then, that my mother had never taught me to hate him.

My father decided to make a trip to talk to my mother. When they met it seemed like they had been together five minutes before, the way they acted. They both asked forgiveness and shared their feelings. They were ready to start all over again. One of their first concerns, though, was religion. My father told my mother, "You keep your religion, and I'll keep mine." He was still very active in the Catholic church, and she in the Pentecostal group.

We went to a party that night, and during the party my father had a heart attack. I knew that was it. I just had that feeling. It was the same feeling I had when I had to look for him. Shortly after they took him to the hospital, he died.

That was a Friday evening. I spent a wretched night on the bus to São Paulo, to tell his relatives. I had a lot of time to think. People would come and talk about saints and tell me to ask a saint to help me. I didn't feel like witnessing, because I was mad at God, at life. I was sad, too. I had broken up with my boyfriend at about the same time.

I came home and continued studying. That was my first year in university and, to my amazement, things were pretty much the same as they had been before. I carried on with everyday life, except when I thought about my father. He hadn't been part of my everyday life, so I didn't really miss him. I wouldn't allow myself to think about him much, because if I did I usually thought God was unfair.

Then my mom began to live with a man who later became her husband. I decided not to go live with her, and went to live with the Thiesens. I lived with them about six months before I went to Montreal and then Texas with the MCC trainee program.

On my return, I finished studying at the university, and then worked doing translations for a light company in Parana. A year later, I had the chance to go back to Montreal because they needed a person who could speak Portuguese and English to work with refugees there. I worked from April 1979 until October 1981, then traveled some, and returned home. Back in Curitiba I worked, studied, and resumed my life.

It was not as it was before though, because I have another view of life. Now I realize it doesn't matter where you're from; you're still a person with needs. I worked a lot with non-Christians in Montreal, and made friends with Muslims, Catholics and Hindus. I guess my main lesson was to accept people where they are.

Cheryl Martin

Wilhelm Hubner

When Wilhelm Hubner and the rest of the baptismal candidates in the village of Fundos Aurora, Brazil, entered the river, people opposed to their baptism threw cow dung and pieces of dead frog into the water. Even so, Wilhelm was confident that he was obeying the will of Christ that his followers should give testimony to their faith by baptism.

Much of the opposition that day arose out of the villagers' own religious background. In the early 1970s there had not been a church of any description in Fundos Aurora, an isolated farming community in the rolling countryside of Santa Catarina state. The Hubner family, like the majority of the German-speaking settlers in the area, would travel twice a year to the Lutheran church in Aurora, a half-day's buggy trip away.

Wilhelm's interest in a closer relationship with God was triggered by the German Bible programs he heard on the radio. In response to listener responses in the Fundos Aurora area, Mennonite preachers came several times to the village to hold evangelistic meetings. Wilhelm attended many of these meetings. He especially enjoyed the music groups which sang in the program. Unlike the lifeless singing in his own church, he felt that this music was full of joy.

Nevertheless, Wilhelm hesitated to do more than simply attend the evangelistic meetings. The Lutheran church in Aurora called the Mennonite preachers false prophets because they advocated a second baptism. Lutherans were warned to stay clear of the new teachings. In addition, Wilhelm's position as treasurer of the local recreation club meant that he had many friends and responsibilities in Fundos Aurora. It would be difficult to go against the traditions and accepted pattern of his community.

Wilhelm recalls one particular week of evangelistic meetings at which J.J. Toews of Canada was speaking. He felt torn between going to the meeting and going to the club dance on Saturday night. In the end, he went to the dance because he had responsibilities there, but as soon as his duty was fulfilled at 12 midnight he wanted to leave. His wife could not understand it; usually Wilhelm liked to party until late into the night.

During this time, Wilhelm was becoming preoccupied with questions about God. He began studying the Bible. Wilhelm wanted to check out for himself everything that was said by the pastors of his own church and by the Mennonite preachers. Sometimes he gave up in confusion because he could not understand the discrepancies and differences between the two.

He gained greater understanding from the daily German Bible program on HCJB, a Christian radio station broadcasting from Quito, Ecuador. One evening the radio pastor read a letter written by Satan worshippers. Afterward the pastor contrasted the Satan worshippers' prayers and songs with those of Christians. This had such an effect on Wilhelm that he immediately knelt down to pray that God would enter his life.

"Are you going to be one of those crazy fanatics too?" his wife Wilma asked when Wilhelm told her about his decision. Despite the skepticism of his family, Wilhelm began taking them with him to the Mennonite Sunday services being held at the school. Within three months Wilma became a Christian as well.

The Hubners' family and friends reacted skeptically to their decision. His father felt that Wilhelm was following the false prophets. It was difficult for the Hubners to go against the wishes of their families and the strong traditions which existed. Even today, no member of Wilhelm's family has made the same decision as he, although several members of Wilma's family have.

Following his decision Wilhelm attended home Bible studies for several months and came to the conclusion that he wanted to be re-baptized. The reactions of his neighbors were vehement. The Sunday of the baptism, a group of people opposed to the baptism gathered on the other side of the river, throwing things into the water and yelling threats at the candidates. "This is the dirtiest water in which I have ever seen people baptized," observed Henry Goerz, a pastor from Curitiba who was conducting the baptism.

Wilhelm's next-door neighbor met him on his way home from the baptism and warned Wilhelm never to come near his land or family again. The ostracism continued for quite a while. A month after his baptism the Hubner's water was poisoned. Fortunately Wilma noticed the water was discolored before she gave her baby its bottle, and no one drank the water.

Despite the opposition, the church in Fundos Aurora grew rapidly. Within the next four years there were between 70 and 80 members. And with time the relationships between members of the community returned to normal, as those opposed realized that the church was growing in spite of their actions, and as the new believers made special efforts to restore friendships. In fact, when the Hubner family moved away from the village two years ago, their community friends were very reluctant to see them go.

Today Wilhelm has a central role in the Mennonite Brethren church in Rio do Sul, where they now live. He has filled executive positions on the church board and currently is an ordained deacon. Although he is now working in town, Wilhelm feels a strong call from God to return to the Aurora area. He remembers the eagerness with which the people

102

would fill meeting halls whenever evangelists would come, and he remembers his own experience of searching for and discovering a vital relationship with God.

Adrienne Wiebe

Paulo Cesar Pareira

In the middle of the night armed policemen on the highway stopped the bus and brought a prisoner on board. The prisoner, a hired killer, sat with his three guards across the aisle from 16-year old Paulo Cesar Pareira. The light over the prisoner's seat was kept on the rest of the night. And all night Paulo could not sleep. He kept looking at the prisoner and thinking of his own life and future. For Paulo, this was a visual lesson arranged by God, illustrating the kind of life he was living.

Over the past two years while his family had been living in the small town of Guiera, Parana, he and an older cousin had got into a pattern of going out in the evenings to see pornographic films and visit bars and prostitutes' houses. Yet when Paulo got home late at night, he would sometimes lie in bed and cry because of the emptiness he felt inside himself. He prayed that God would become real to him; that he would actually see God and feel some peace in his life.

Although they did not know exactly what was happening in Paulo's life, his parents were concerned about him and often brought religious books home for him from their Catholic retreats and Bible studies. Paulo especially remembers one of the books, which was written as if the narrator was a person living with Jesus during his life on earth. "I read that book many times," he says, "and I cried every time I read the part about Jesus' death. I didn't know that he died for me. I didn't understand it."

At about this time Paulo's parents decided to move back to Curitiba where the rest of their children still lived. But Paulo, tied down to his job as a disc jockey, stayed in Guiera for another month. "I really lived it up that month I lived alone," says Paulo. "I had decided that this was the way my life would always be and that there was no possibility of changing it."

It was on the trip to Curitiba to join his parents that he saw the prisoner on the bus. This scene affected him so deeply that he decided to try to change his life. He also wanted to help his father, who was in financial difficulties after his recent switch in jobs.

Paulo immediately got a job with the state radio station, and continued to go to school full-time. Yet he still felt lonely and empty. The small apartment in which his family lived was cramped. He had few friends in Curitiba. His growing feelings of emptiness and his lack of friends and goals brought him to the point of considering suicide. Several times as he walked home from school he would close his eyes as he crossed streets, waiting to be hit by a car.

Hope came unexpectedly one week when Paulo was demonstrating radio operation at a public exhibition. There he met Rachel Friesen, who was working at a booth representing the Federal Technical School. They became friends immediately. Paulo felt that at last he had found a friend in whom he could confide and who understood him. Rachel encouraged him to continue life with hope.

As their friendship grew, Paulo learned that Rachel was a Christian. She invited him to a retreat for young people being held at ISBIM, the Mennonite Brethren Bible Institute and Seminary in Curitiba. Eager to go, Paulo managed to switch his working hours with someone so that he could be there at least Saturday evening and Sunday.

"Saturday evening after supper there was a chapel," recalls Paulo, "but I didn't want to go. I had the feeling that there was a monster or a live spirit in the room where they were gathering. I was too afraid to go in, so I waited outside for two hours while they had their meeting."

Even so, Paulo returned the next day to enjoy an afternoon of volleyball and soccer. When it came time for chapel, Paulo says, "I decided to go. The night before they had just been singing and talking, so I thought it couldn't be that bad. I would simply face whatever it was that was in there.

"I remember the first song they sang. It was about how God was a God of love. The people sang with such joy that I wanted to know why. I didn't listen to the speaker much, I just looked at the people. I wanted the free joy that I saw on their faces. Talking with them later I discovered that it was Jesus who was making them so happy.

"I didn't make any decisions then," Paulo continued, "I didn't know I had to. But after being empty for so long, I didn't want to lose the happiness I felt among those people."

Eager to learn more, Paulo began attending Jardim das Americas Mennonite Brethren Church. Pat Klassen, a missionary who also attends the church, notes, "Paulo even went to the Wednesday evening Bible studies even though there were no other young people his age, just older adults."

Two months later Paulo made a conscious decision to accept Jesus into his life. "Marcos, one of my friends from school asked me how I knew I was saved," says Paulo, "and I sort of choked up. I said I thought it was because of the good things I did. But Marcos explained to me that a person was saved by personal faith in Jesus Christ. After we prayed together, Marcos told me to go home, go into my room alone, close the door, kneel down and pray to accept Christ into my life. I was so impressed by Marcos' authority and I wanted this so badly that, I just rushed home and prayed."

Paulo made that decision in 1980. In reflecting back on his search, he is convinced that nothing in his life was coincidental. Rather, he feels that circumstances and people were all helping to reveal God to him.   *Andrienne Wiebe*

Jorge and Luci Perdonsin

Jorge and Luci Perdonsin could tell story after story of God's provision in their lives—if they chose to sit still long enough to do it.

The Perdonsins are currently very active in pastoral and outreach ministries in the Portuguese Mennonite Brethren churches of Francisco Beltrão and São Lourenço, rural towns in the Brazilian state of Parana. Like many pastor couples in Brazil, the Perdonsins find that faith living is a concrete affair, whether it means trusting God for a new battery for the old VW they use in their itinerant ministry, or waiting for a skeleton salary and occasional gifts from the people they serve. The story of their conversions, wedding and call to service shows how that faith has had opportunity to grow.

For Jorge, the pilgrimage goes back to when he was four. A member of the Uberaba Mennonite Brethren church in Curitiba had invited him and his older brother Paulo to attend Sunday school. When the boys told their mother what happened at the services she began going also, and very soon decided to follow Christ.

"That's when the problems began," says Jorge. "My dad didn't want any of us to go to church, and we boys watched fighting happening in our home because of the church. Mom wanted to be baptized, but Dad wouldn't let her. She waited through several baptisms at the church but before the year was out was baptized without our father knowing it.

"The fighting went on for about 17 years," continues Jorge. "After much pleading my father finally consented to let my mother take a job as cook for the Mennonite Brethren Bible Institute. Through this contact with students, pastors, and missionaries my father's resistance was gradually worn down. The situation at home began improving."

Jorge, meanwhile, became president of the church youth group, although he had not yet joined the church. Following junior high school he thought of attending the Bible institute but was told he was too young. The desire faded and he began working while continuing his studies. When the pastor invited Jorge to be baptized he repeatedly resisted, and finally decided to leave the church altogether.

Following high school Jorge enlisted in the military. He served in the honored presidential guard in Brasilia, and worked his way up to become commander of the guard at the National Congress.

"I had a good position, a good salary, and was seeing some of my dreams come true," he says, "but I still wasn't happy. So I returned home and got back an old job as a mechanic at a print shop."

Jorge also decided to break up with the Christian girl he had been dating the past three years and began dating a pretty, popular girl named Luci, whom he had met at work.

"I made sure to get a girlfriend who lived the kind of life I wanted," he says. "I began going to dances and parties, just to be with her. But I didn't feel at liberty to participate. Inside I felt something lacking. There was a light inside me which reminded me I had gone forward at an evangelistic campaign and accepted the Lord when I was 15."

In spite of Jorge's efforts to break away from a Christian upbringing, Luci remembers that he was different from the others she had dated. "I didn't know he was a Christian, but saw something different in him," she recalls.

Life in Luci's family had been made difficult by fighting among siblings and a father who hid his money instead of using it for food. Luci began babysitting for neighbors at age nine, and started cleaning houses at 12.

"I came home at night and cried because I wanted something different for my family," she says. "I didn't realize I was praying, but I told God, 'I want to be someone in life, and help my family improve.'" Luci looked to both Catholic and Spiritist churches for happiness, but neither satisfied her.

"When I was older I tried to find peace for my agitation at discos and parties. I would stay until morning with my two brothers, and while I was there I was happy, and could forget my troubles. But when I left, all the troubles returned."

She got a job at the print shop where Jorge worked, and they began dating. After two months Jorge told Luci he wanted to talk seriously to her.

"I thought he wanted to break up," recalls Luci, "because he said he wanted to become engaged, but then added that he was an evangelical. All I could think to say was, 'This Sunday I'm going to your church.'"

Jorge, however, had waited to mention his Christianity until after he proposed because he was afraid Luci would refuse to marry him. He was surprised that she wanted to visit his church, but took her "just to show her what it was like."

Luci continued attending church with Jorge, despite her family's taunts. She hoped to impress Jorge's mother, and enjoyed eating Sunday dinner at Jorge's house.

"I began to see the difference between Jorge's home and mine," she says. "I felt as if I was in heaven at his house, and in hell when I returned home."

Jorge, meanwhile, felt things had gone far enough. He decided they would go to one more church service, then quit. That service happened to be during an evangelistic campaign, and a turning point in Luci's life.

"Because of the message I saw all the pollution in my life," Luci says. "I also saw the solution for my life and the problems of my family. After Christ entered my life I didn't feel like I had to impress Jorge or his mother anymore. I wanted to serve God. I had been praying to God before but didn't realize that I hadn't let him act. Now I wanted him to participate in my life."

Jorge's initial response was different. "What a surprise that was," he says. "She began talking about being baptized, and wanted me to be baptized also. I thought, 'What's happening to me? I wanted to leave the church and now I'm more involved than before.' I noticed, though, that God had really held onto my hand, so finally I decided to follow him faithfully. After we were engaged we were baptized together."

Not long after, Jorge's eyesight began failing. Finally he entered the hospital for a cornea transplant. While lying in bed with his eyes bandaged he had time to think.

"I discovered that all the time I thought I was doing God's will I was following dead ends. I remembered God had called me at one time and decided to accept God's call."

At a church Missions Day in October 1974 Jorge and Luci dedicated their lives to full-time Christian service. They were married in December, and began attending the Mennonite Brethren Bible Institute three months later.

Those were rough years for the young couple. The man who had offered to pay for Jorge's tuition experienced bankruptcy, so Jorge began doing maintenance for the school. His salary, however, was not enough both to pay tuition and provide for the needs of the family, which by the second year included a son.

Jorge and Luci began asking God to provide, and he did. One man at church regularly passed them money enclosed in a warm handshake. Women would bring Luci a can of oil or a bag of rice at church ladies' meetings.

After five years of working and studying Jorge graduated from the Bible institute. He and Luci told the conference president they were ready to go anywhere the Lord called them. Three churches had extended invitations: the Center Church in Curitiba, the Bage church farther south, and the Santo Antonio Church in São Paulo, a city of 13 million.

"Center Church had a very nice parsonage," says Luci, "so it was tempting. The Bage church was in a farming community so we would have been given a pair of turkeys, some chickens and cow. It was a struggle to face the prospect of having all those physical provisions after our Bible institute years.

"But that night I couldn't sleep. Jorge, too, was going through the same struggle, although I didn't know it. At breakfast we both concluded those weren't the Lord's will. We felt we should go to São Paulo."

The parsonage at Santo Antonio, however, was another experience of growing in faith for Jorge and Luci. The house consisted of two former Sunday school rooms with broken windows, no electricity and no running water.

"That was the first time I became angry with God," admits Luci. "I had to carry 18 buckets of water down the stairs to do the laundry. My first prayer was for running water. When I told a church member I was praying for that, he said they had been waiting 20 years for the city to put in water. However, within three months we had water." Prayers for everything from chairs to a kitchen sink followed, and the Perdonsins' needs were met.

Near the beginning of the four and a half years at Santo Antonio, Jorge and Luci also had to trust God to deal with tensions within the church. "Some families were against us at first," says Luci, "and one made a petition for us to leave. So Jorge said, 'This is no good. Let's pray.' At every meal and before bed, we prayed for that family. One day the man of the family came to Jorge, hugged him and said, 'What I thought before I don't think now.' He began to help and became vice president of the church."

São Paulo was not to become the Perdonsins' permanent home, however. In addition to pastoral responsibilities, Jorge served on a Convention committee which, for two years, dealt with the pastoral problems of a church in the rural town of São Lourenço. "Through this God gave me compassion for that church," says Jorge. "But we didn't want to leave São Paulo. The church was going well, and we had come through so much."

When Conference leaders invited Jorge to pastor the churches at São Lourenço and nearby Fransisco Beltrão, he reluctantly agreed to visit the area. "God gave me a new vision that there was much to do there," Jorge says. "But always the question returned. 'What about the church in São Paulo?'

"Then God gave me the idea to raise up a new leader in the Convention. I decided that if a certain man in our church would agree to give up his secular job to pastor the church it would indicate that God wanted me to go to the other churches. I talked to the man, without telling him of my decision, and he simply accepted. I was overwhelmed."

"Now we're here," Jorge continues, "and there's a new worker in the Convention. The Lord is blessing the work at Santo Antonio, and the people are satisfied with the leader."

Jorge and Luci moved to the town of Francisco Beltrão in April 1983 and have since been following a busy schedule of visitation, broadcasting local radio programs, and acting as a resource to lay leaders in the churches.

Unlike many other Convention pastors, who have had to take up part-time jobs to support their families, Jorge and Luci have opted to live on the salary they receive from the church members, plus a small Convention subsidy and contributions of food from congregation members.

They feel, along with the other Convention pastoral couples, that lack of resources to support pastors is the biggest problem currently facing the Brazilian churches. Jorge envisions resolving the resource problem—which he feels also contributes to the shortage of pastors—by having one pastor supervise several supporting churches, each led by strong lay people. He is already operating under this system with his two congregations and three outreach points, but hopes to strengthen local leadership so he can eventually take further studies. *Cheryl Martin*

uruguay

URUGUAY

Population:	3 million
Capital:	Montevideo
Language:	Spanish
Religions:	Roman Catholic (60%), non-religious (31%), Protestant (1.9%) (Evangelicals: 1.5%)

Mennonite Brethren Conference of Uruguay: 170 members in 7 churches and 4 extension groups.
Missions/Services ministries: Bible teaching, pastoral resource ministries, church planting

Mennonite Brethren church planting in Uruguay was built on the work of two hostels in Montevideo run by Mennonite Central Committee and the then MB General Conference Board of Welfare. The hostels were started to serve Mennonite settlers who had immigrated to the country in 1930s and 40s, particularly young men and women coming from the colonies to find work in the city. In 1968, the first Missions/Services workers, Dan and Elsie Wirsche, continued evangelistic ministries to Spanish-speaking Montevideans which had emerged out of the hostel programs.

As some Mennonites emigrated from Uruguay, the Spanish church grew — mostly in Montevideo, but also in Jan Javier and Pando. Through the financial assistance of Missions/Services, a seaside camp, Villa Maranatha, was opened in 1979 and has proved an integral asset in youth outreach and church renewal. Also key to the conference's development has been its Bible institute in Montevideo, which draws full and part-time students from the churches. Both at the institute and in the churches, Uruguayan initiative in evangelism has been strong; films, literature and evangelistic preaching have been used extensively.

Lila Radionov

Lila Radionov thought she had everything planned to live happily and quietly for the rest of her life in her hometown of San Javier, northwestern Uruguay. At 34, she had led a somewhat transient life, working for the past 15 years as a domestic servant in several other cities. Now she was going to settle down, live with her mother and open her own photography business.

"However, that was not God's plan," she says now, as she looks back. In 1979, three years after her return to San Javier, her mother died. "The loneliness after her death was tremendous," she remembers. "My mother had been the center of my life." She might have committed suicide had it not been for one friend, Maria, who helped her through the mourning period. Lila often spent the night at Maria's house.

A few months later, in February of 1980, the Mennonite Brethren church in San Javier held an evangelistic campaign featuring Albert Enns of Paraguay as speaker. After attending these meetings, Lila started going to the church on Sundays. "I began learning of the salvation and love of God," says Lila, "and I also learned that Christians are to pardon their enemies." But she was not yet ready to make a personal commitment.

At the time, the military government of Uruguay was cracking down on persons suspected of anti-government activities. Since San Javier had a high percentage of people, like Lila, with Russian immigrant roots, that town was particularly suspect, and some 30 people were arrested.

In May, the soldiers raided Lila's house looking for arms, returning four days later to arrest her and take her to a jail 40 miles away. Maria and two others were also taken at the same time.

For 10 days she and nine other people were held and left completely alone, none of them knowing why they were there. Lila was on the verge of a nervous collapse, but she was given tranquilizers to calm her.

It was in jail that Lila made her decision to follow Christ. She prayed constantly that God would help her through the ordeal. Remembering what she had learned about forgiving one's enemies, she also prayed for the soldiers holding her.

When she was finally called for interrogation, Lila was asked about her relationship with Maria, whose husband was one of the leaders of the Tupamaros, a left-wing opposition group especially strong in Uruguay before the 1973 coup which put the present government into power. However, nothing could be found that linked Lila to any subversive activity.

The San Javier church was overjoyed to see her return from detention, and welcomed the news of her decision to become a Christian.

That October, when the weather had become warm, Lila was baptized in a local river.

In 1981, the Lord led Lila to begin studying at the Mennonite Brethren Training Center, the Bible institute run by the Mennonite Brethren conference of Uruguay. Learning how to study was an initial challenge, for she had had only three years of schooling. And living in a dormitory with a group of younger students also taught her much about Christian living.

After her graduation at the end of 1983, Lila was intending to return to San Javier to settle down quietly in her house—but she remembered what happened last time she had a similar plan and God had a totally different one. So this time Lila left her plans with a lot of leeway for God to guide her in his own way.

Adrienne Wiebe

Maurice and Henrietta Sastre

When economic depression and political instability hit Uruguay in the early 1970s, Maurice and Henrietta Sastre could no longer afford to operate their small convenience store in Montevideo. Like many Uruguayans, they went across the huge Roi de la Plata estuary to find work in Argentina.

In Buenos Aires, the capital, the Sastres did find employment as caretakers of an apartment building—but they also began to discover a God who would meet the many other needs they had.

Two Pentecostal missionaries living in their building would often chat with Henrietta in the hallway, inviting her to come to their church with them. Henrietta always refused, saying she was a Catholic.

The daughter of a village water carrier, she had grown up in a poor family of 10 children in rural Uruguay. They had been a happy family, believing in God and going to the Catholic church as often as they could.

But her faithfulness waned when she divorced her first husband, an alcoholic whom she had married at age 16. God had even less room in her life when she left her three children in the care of their grandmother and worked in a Montevideo factory to support them.

Maurice, Henrietta's second husband, had also been a devout Catholic at one time. But at age 39 he had an experience with the church which left him bitter against it. He had been looking for a priest to perform the last rites for his dying uncle, and all five priests he asked were either too busy or too tired to come. This made him feel sure that priests were not Christ's representatives on earth after all, and he quit going to church.

Now middle-aged and living in Buenos Aires, the Sastres were struggling to live without God.

One day Henrietta intercepted one of the missionaries on her way to her Bible study and prayer meeting, and asked if the group could pray for the healing of a chest pain she had had for many years. What could she lose? To her surprise, the pain began disappearing the next day when the missionary came by to assure her that the group had prayed for her. At that point, Henrietta was convinced of God's power.

Her first service at the Pentecostal church was an emotional one; she sang and prayed and wept. The pastor and members of the church prayed for her, and she began putting her trust in God, releasing the tension and worry which had plagued her since her first marriage.

In 1981 the Sastres moved back to Montevideo, again followed by economic difficulties. They could not find work, and the people living in the two little apartments behind their house would not pay their rent. Maurice came close to having a nervous breakdown.

But eventually, God spoke powerfully to him through the example of Henrietta's life and the teaching of the Penarol Mennonite Brethren Church which they had begun attending. He realized that there was nothing he could do except put everything in the Lord's hands and trust him. Since he became a Christian, the renters have been paying the rent, which provides a very meager income while they look for work.

"I don't think anyone else could do it," says Maurice, "but the Lord has taken care of us and blessed us. When Christian brothers and sisters come to visit, we always have been able to serve them something to eat."

Today, Maurice and Henrietta are anxious to see the Lord help others in the same way. They recently started having weekly Bible studies and prayer meetings in their home in La Valleja, a poor neighborhood of *ranchitos* (Spanish for shacks made of scrap materials).

They and other members of the Penarol church would like this "annex" to grow into a full-fledged church in Uruguay's Mennonite Brethren conference. Already, outdoor evangelistic meetings have been held in the neighborhood. The Penarol group is also talking about ways of helping the La Valleja residents in physical ways too—making their houses more water-proof, serving hot milk and a snack to children in the Sunday School, and finding a doctor and a lawyer to work in the area.

Eventually the Sastres would like to work full-time for the church. Maurice has been taking courses at the Mennonite Brethren Bible Institute in the city to help him in whatever service God calls him to. But perhaps more than anything else, it is Henrietta and Maurice's own experience of placing their burdens on the Lord which has enabled them to offer to others the joy and peace of living with Christ.

Adrienne Wiebe

Pedro Arioni

Before he found Christ, Pedro Arioni's life was one big obsession to become rich. Today, as a pastor of one of the four Mennonite Brethren churches in Montevideo, he has a new passion—serving the Lord.

Pedro's drive for wealth was something that seemed to run in the family. The Arionis, a rich industrial family in Italy, had immigrated to Uruguay in 1940, and had become firmly established in Montevideo's business world. Pedro's father, the youngest son in the family, had everything going for him; he had studied medicine, veterinary science and engineering, and he could speak five languages.

But everything changed when, to the disgrace of the family, he fell in love with and married one of the servant girls, a simple Uruguayan from the countryside. Rejection by the family, poor money management and laziness soon drove the couple and their children to poverty. Even so, Pedro grew up feeling that he was an upper-class person—that he was not meant to be poor and that someday he would be rich.

From the time he began playing soccer at age five until he entered the major leagues as a teenager, he had dreams that an athletic career would open the door to wealth. However, that dream was abruptly shattered when he broke his leg at age 20. The injury took two years to heal.

Meanwhile, Pedro's sister had been going to the Sunday school classes at the Penarol Mennonite Brethren Church in their neighborhood. With her encouragement, he started attending, and he soon made an initial decision to follow Christ. His jovial outgoing nature quickly made him a popular storyteller, musician and Sunday school teacher in the church.

But all this time Pedro continued an internal struggle with the desire to be rich. Since playing soccer could no longer make him wealthy, he decided that music might be the way. He began studying the guitar, hoping to become a concert musician. For five years, while working full time with the government utility company and raising a family with his wife Olira, he was devoted to his guitar. He would often practice through the night.

But again, something seemed to be working against Pedro's plans. First, he had problems with the tendons in his left hand, and eventually had to go through surgery. Then his other hand developed an allergy to the guitar strings, which made his fingers bleed.

None of the doctors he consulted could identify what the problem was. After talking with Pedro, one doctor said, "If this is a problem between you and God, then there's nothing we doctors can do about it." Disappointed, Pedro had to give up his dreams of wealth and fame as a concert guitarist.

However, his old dream of soccer renown awoke with new energy when he noticed people praising the soccer skills of his two sons. His fortune would now be in his children. For four years he trained his sons to be excellent soccer players, instilling in them the desire to win and to always put their own ambitions first.

"I always thought God and I were good friends," says Pedro. "My prayers were like conversations with God. I was very demanding, telling God exactly what I wanted: one tall son and one short one. In soccer, sometimes height is important, and sometimes it's shortness and speed."

Of course, it was a one-way "friendship" with God. However, that began to change during his enrollment at the

Mennonite Brethren Bible Institute in 1981. The real turning point came one day when he happened to read a passage from Hebrews 13: "Keep your lives free from the love of money and be content with what you have, because God has said, 'Never will I leave you; never will I forsake you.'"

"I realized then that I had always been controlled by my ambitions and had been unhappy," Pedro remembers. "Now I wanted to live in peace. I finally decided to put everything into God's hands."

Within three days of this decision, the stomach pains he had suffered much of his life disappeared. The joviality which he had always shown outwardly now sprang from a growing joy deep within him.

At the end of June, 1983, he and Olira were ordained to the ministry in the El Faro Mennonite Brethren Church, where they had been serving informally since 1980. The new assignment promises to be a challenge for the Arionis; shortly before their ordination the El Faro Church had moved several blocks to a new location, sending attendance into a sharp decline.

Yet Pedro has faith that God will help him in his new task of building the church. "I have gained much experience from my struggle with wealth," he says, "and this helps me now in my preaching and pastoring. Since God has liberated me from my old desires, I am now learning to lose my own life for the work of the Lord—and in the end I know I will gain."

Adrienne Wiebe

japan

JAPAN

Population:	118,450,000
Capital:	Tokyo
Language:	Japanese
Religions:	Buddhist and Shinto or offshoots (95%), Christian (3%). (Evangelicals: 0.3%)

Mennonite Brethren Conference of Japan: 1400 members, 16 churches, 7 mission churches.

Missions/Services ministries: Church planting, seminary instruction, Christian education publishing, and evangelistic English classes.

Japan has traditionally been a difficult country to penetrate with the good news of Christ. Strong family traditions, rooted in Buddhist and Shinto culture, make conversion to Christianity a major transition. However, the Mennonite Brethren have maintained a steady growth since missionaries began church planting in Osaka in 1950, following the postwar reconstruction done by Mennonite Central Committee.

In the subsequent 34 years, Missions/Services' pattern has been to send church planters into major urban centers — Osaka, Nagoya, Hyogo Ken, Tokuyama and Hiroshima — to establish churches, which are then taken over by Japanese pastors. Friendship evangelism and relationship-building have been key to that process.

Since the Japanese MB conference was formed in 1967, evangelistic work of Missions/Services has been conducted in close consultation with it, and the Japanese have themselves taken a greater role in church planting. The conference currently has its own missionary working under Wycliffe Bible Translators.

Ikuko Kinoshita

"The flowers and trees looked different to me. Suddenly everything was beautiful and bright, for now I knew the creator." This simple statement of the transforming power of God is the climax of Ikuko Kinoshita's testimony. Now a member of the Senri Mennonite Brethren church in Osaka, she shares freely of her struggle to find God.

For Mrs. Kinoshita life had been easy. She had had a happy childhood, her family was wealthy and she never had to worry about anything. She was young, recently married and just beginning a new life in China where her husband was a prosperous businessman.

Then World War II broke out and the bottom dropped out from beneath them. Forced to flee from China, her family left everything behind, returned to Japan and tried to pick up the broken pieces of their life despite a ruined economy.

A year later, their six-year-old son died of dysentery. "It was a real shock to us," Mrs. Kinoshita related. "He had been sick for only one night and in the morning he was dead!" Shortly after that Mrs. Kinoshita discovered that she had cancer, but through massive surgery, doctors were able to arrest it. As she looks back now, she believes that the Lord miraculously preserved her life. But back then?

"My parents were Buddhist, and as a child I remember worshipping at our family altar every day. Sometimes I even accompanied my father on trips to the temple. But all of this was just ritual. I don't remember ever having a belief in any sort of God. After we were married, we didn't even practice the rituals anymore.

"Yet, even in my childhood I always felt that a human being was more than just a body. We have a heart and a soul too. It is what's inside that is important because happiness is something on the inside, not on the outside."

It was not until years later that Mrs Kinoshita heard about the one true God through the help of a neighbor. She accepted an invitation to attend a neighborhood cottage meeting where two things particularly impressed her. "I liked the way the group sang so beautifully together," she said, "but more than that, I was really moved by the warm hearts of missionaries Roland and Ann Wiens, who were also at the meeting. As a result, she began to read the Bible her friend had given her and continued attending the meetings.

"Even though I couldn't understand it all, I came to realize that God knows everything," she says, recalling the struggles that followed. "He knows about even the tiniest sins and he hates them. At first, I thought that maybe God was too strict. After all, I was a good person, not a sinner; I was an honest person, not a criminal. Yet the Bible said that I wasn't good enough. Maybe God hates me, I thought. Maybe he won't accept me. That was when I began to understand why Christ was on the cross. It was for me! In John 3:16 I read that whoever believes on the Lord Jesus Christ will be saved. When I read this, I believed. That was in 1963; I was 43 years old."

The change which came about in her life was like going from darkness into bright light, according to Mrs. Kinoshita's description. Her husband was the first to notice the change. Once a constant worrier about money and health, she began to display a quiet trust in God. Once a total atheist, she became a faithful witness of Christ, working to bring her husband to a knowledge of God.

The task was not an easy one, for it is the duty of a

Japanese woman to obey her husband. To make him see that the new way she had found was the only one to follow had to be done tactfully, without injuring his pride. He would have to discover it for himself. So she encouraged him to search on his own by giving him gifts of printed scripture verses and leaving a Bible on his desk in the hope that he would read it. Two years later, her patience and prayers were rewarded as her husband also believed and was baptized.

Now the Kinoshita home is open to continue the spread of the gospel through cottage meetings. Having heard Mrs. Kinoshita's story, many come to her for advice and counselling and she leads them to a knowledge of the creator. "People come looking for peace," she explains. "As I understand God's love more and more, I am happy to teach them about him. Are you familiar with II Corinthians 5:17? I have seen it work. 'If anyone is in Christ, he is a new creation; the old has gone, the new has come!'"

Carolyn Hamm

Junichi Fujino

The charm hangs on a chain around the neck. In a small vinyl bag next to the skin is a piece of paper folded into a four-inch square. On it is written the Japanese character meaning "light." This charm acts like a radio receiver drawing power from God. The wearer can then bring healing to others as the power radiates its light through the palms of his hands. Junichi Fujino saw it work when his mother had been healed of tuberculosis. He himself had practised the rite on others and they had been healed.

Now a pastor of a Mennonite Brethren Church in Osaka, Japan, Junichi Fujino once embraced a heretical sect of Shintoism known as "World Messianity." The group emphasized healing and claimed that salvation would start in the east and spread to all the world. It was only after the struggles and uncertainties of his university days that he found Christianity.

He had initially gone to university to study science believing, as his religion taught, that someday science and religion would harmonize. In his final year, however, he was attracted to a lecture called "Beyond Science," by a certain Dr. Herbert Mitchell. Invited to the lecture by Mennonite Brethren missionary Dr. Harry Friesen, the NASA scientist ended his lecture by speaking of Christ and salvation. Since all who attended the lecture were invited to the Friesens for coffee, Fujino joined them and began asking questions.

"At that time I had no doubts about my religion," he stated. "I talked and preached about it to others. I was preparing to become a foreign missionary for it. In fact, my university education was suffering because I was working so hard for the religion. I was working for my salvation.

"When I discussed this with Dr. Mitchell, however, I suddenly had the feeling that he personally knew God and I did not. When he talked about a salvation which did not depend on works, I decided that there must be another salvation than the one I knew about."

Prior to this, Fujino had had a few chance exposures to Christianity, giving him the impression that Christianity was very narrow for claiming to be the only true religion. But after Dr. Mitchell's lecture, he was interested in the Bible. "I wanted to know the truth; I was thirsty," he explained.

One day he met Dr. Friesen accidentally at the train station and told him that he was interested in studying the Bible. Friesen invited him to the Sunday evening English and Bible classes at their home and Fujino began attending the meeting.

Every week he brought questions to discuss with Dr. Friesen and every week he searched for answers. He was perplexed at the creation/evolution issue but after much studying came to the conclusion that "creation was more scientific than evolution." In his reading he discovered that Biblical prophecy had been fulfilled 100%. For him, this established the fact that the God of the Bible is the true God. Next, he discovered that the center of the Bible is Christ; he learned that the most important message of the Bible is to believe in Christ for salvation. "I couldn't accept it," he said. "I was still tied to my previous beliefs."

Realizing his need, Dr. Friesen began meeting with Fujino every week for two to three hours. While Fujino asked questions, Harry tried to answer them. Among other things, he explained to Fujino that God is always one step behind you. If you turn to him and say, "I accept salvation," he will save you.

Fujino described his struggle: "At first I tried to bring the two religions together, but it didn't work. I realized that I had to believe. On March 13, 1979, I made my decision. The moment I finished my prayer to accept Christ, I felt something enter into me. That feeling was the assurance that I had been saved."

Fujino didn't want to continue with his old religion, but by this time, he had committed himself to attend the World Messianity seminary and his integrity compelled him to follow through with this commitment. "The lectures were boring." he remembered. "They were all on doctrines that I already knew were false. I knew that no one in that religion knew God or had salvation. The best times were when I was reading the Bible and when I went back to the Ishibashi church every Sunday."

Behind the scenes, the Friesens, the Christians meeting in their home and the members of the Ishibashi church were praying him through. For seven months he struggled with his Christianity in the environment of his old religion. "Those were transitional days for me," he recalled. "But it was during this year that I finally realized that World Messianity was from Satan; its healing power was satanic, the same as sorcery."

In 1981, the Lord called Fujino into the full time ministry. Upon the completion of his studies at the Evangelical Biblical Seminary (Mennonite Brethren) in Osaka in March, 1983, he took over the pastorate at the Kuzuha Mennonite Brethren church in northern Osaka. "My goal," he concluded, "is to build the church and raise my family according to the Word."

Carolyn Hamm

Hideko Ogata

"War changed everything in Korea. We Japanese had to leave in a hurry. My bags were just too heavy and too full. The only solution was to throw away my statue of Buddha. I did, and for years I regretted it—until . . ."

Korea was the only home Hideko Ogata had known until the Japanese were forced to evacuate at the close of World War 2. Her parents were dead, she had no money or food, and now she was forced to go to a strange country alone and there find and care for an invalid brother. And, worst of all, her Buddha was gone. On what could she rely?

Hideko decided that the solution was independence. She moved to a small mining town on the island of Kyushu, got a job with a coal company, and there set up a home where she could care for her brother. When he miraculously started walking a year later, Hideko was free to be married. Now she could rely on her husband.

Then her brother was diagnosed as having tuberculosis and was admitted to a hospital in Hiroshima. Unable to help from her new home in Osaka, Hideko was heavily burdened with guilt as the years passed. For 21 years her brother was in the hospital.

While there he heard about Christianity through the regular visits of pastors. His letters to Hideko always mentioned the Bible and Christianity. Summarizing her reaction to this strange turn of events, Hideko says, "I had read somewhere that it was shameful if someone reached 50 and still had nothing on which to rely. Although I wasn't interested in Christianity, I was glad to hear that he had found something to rely on. It made him happier than he was before."

Six years later, Hideko received a call from Hiroshima saying that her brother was in critical condition. As she rushed to be with him in his last days, she chided herself for not having done more for him. When she arrived, she found her brother praying with a friend. "I prayed too," she recalls, "even though I didn't know to whom I was directing my prayers."

Hideko was impressed with her brother's attitude towards death. "Christianity has really done something for him," she thought. "His condition is poor, yet he is cheering me up." When he died, Hideko was responsible for the funeral. Her husband suggested that a church funeral would be appropriate, since her brother had been a Christian. But they had no contacts with churches.

Then Hideko remembered that she had once passed a church while out walking her dog. It was the Sojiji Mennonite Brethren Church in northern Osaka. At first she was hesitant to ask for help there. "It was New Year's—everyone was busy and I was a stranger," she explains. But to her surprise, everyone was kind and willing to help.

"I heard about life after death for the first time at the funeral," she says. "That impressed me. I had always felt sorry for my brother having to be in the hospital for so long and finally dying. Now I thought that if he was in heaven, maybe his life hadn't been so bad after all."

She and her husband continued attending church services after the funeral and, step by step, she began to believe. But when the pastor suggested that she be baptized, she couldn't go through with it. "I was afraid," she admits. "I knew that Jesus had died for my sins and forgiven them, but I couldn't accept it. I had committed the big sin of leaving my brother in the hospital for 21 years and not looking after him the way I should have. How could that be forgiven?"

One day, one of her brother's Christian friends wrote her a letter and explained that someone had died so she could live. If her brother hadn't been in the hospital, he wrote, he probably never would have become a Christian and neither would she. God had put him in the hospital so that they could hear the gospel.

"Then I understood God's plan. The verse about the kernel of wheat having to die in order to live became my favorite. My brother's death had introduced me to life. God cared and I could truly rely on him," she shares, recalling the experience. "That's when I was able to burn my new figure of Buddha without regret. I realized that years ago, when I had thrown away my Buddha, I had done the right thing."

Carolyn Hamm

Hajimu Fujii

Those who are open are the ones whom God can use and the ones through whom God can speak. Throughout his life, Hajimu Fujii has been open and willing to try new things. Now an auditor at the Mennonite Brethren Evangelical Bible Seminary in Osaka, he gives his reason for attending school as follows: "I have a thirst for the Word; I need to learn so that I may be equipped to proclaim the gospel. I need to prepare myself in case the Lord should call me to the ministry."

Fujii is preparing himself in more ways than one. Wanting to begin a new church fellowship, he and his family have bought a combination home and pharmacy arranged in such a way as to have a room that will lend itself for use as a large meeting place. Previously, one needed to have a church building in order to begin a Christian fellowship in Japan. Perhaps the house fellowship with lay leaders is a pattern for the future. Fujii is open to these new ideas.

It was this same open-minded attitude which first brought Fujii into contact with Christianity. After months of struggling to make it on his own in a pharmacy business, he embraced a sect of Buddhism which emphasizes sin and man's need to rely on something outside himself for salvation. Aware of his inability to always do good things, Fujii was convinced of his sin and embraced belief in the imaginary force of *Amida* as a means of overcoming it.

Yet his interest in religion was not satisfied just because

he thought he had found the truth. He was still interested in truth as other people saw it. One day, while negotiating a business deal with a certain doctor, Fujii got into a discussion about religion. Although not a Christian the doctor claimed, "If you are interested in religion, Christianity is the best one." Although Fujii could not believe it, the things that the doctor shared concerning Christ and the Bible were so forceful that Fujii was immediately intrigued. "I was interested in the truth—I wanted to know what was right and what was wrong," Fujii explains. "I was open to hear what the doctor had to say."

As a result Fujii began reading books about Christianity. In a book by C.S. Lewis he read about the soul of man being more eternal than the nations. Curious about this statement, Fujii decided to go back to the source of this new religion—the Bible.

He was impressed by biblical teachings on lifestyle. "Upon understanding verses like those about the birds of the air and the lilies of the field, I began to see my life for what it really was. Living only to make money was miserable," he shares, recalling his initial leading. "As a result I tried to live according to the Bible. I shortened my work hours and took more time for my family and other important things." By trying to follow the biblical pattern, Fujii and his wife assumed that they must be Christians.

Four years later, they decided to attend a Billy Graham crusade in Osaka. "Since we were already Christians," Fujii says, remembering the event, "we thought we would take along my wife's mother so that she too could become a Christian. Were we ever in for a surprise!"

Fujii recalled the experience at the crusade: "The power in that man was amazing, but it was what he said about Christ and salvation that really impressed me. Going to that meeting changed our lives. The Lord had sent us there."

A short time later, as a result of contacts at the crusade, Pastor Kurokawa of the Tsuchiyama Mennonite Brethren

Church visited the Fujii home. He was the first real Christian the Fujiis had ever met.

Fujii's interest in Christianity grew and, as he read more and more books, he discussed his questions with Pastor Kurokawa. "The problem of creation was a big question because I had been taught evolution as fact," he shares. "I also wanted to know the truth about the Holy Spirit." Sometimes the pastor would answer his questions directly and other times he would collect the information for Fujii and let him discover the answers on his own.

Fujii was elated. "As my questions were resolved, it was like ice melting and I could see the image of Jesus in my heart," he shares. After several months, both Fujii and his wife were sure of their salvation. On April 18, 1981, they were baptized. He was not afraid to try something new and it paid off. "Now I know the truth and I am satisfied," he concludes.

Carolyn Hamm

indonesia

INDONESIA

Population: 153 million
Capital: Jakarta
Language: Indonesian (official), local dialects
Religions: Muslim (87%), Christian (10%), Hindu (2%). (Evangelicals: 4.4%)

Indonesian Muria Synod (Mennonite): 5,000 baptized members in 18 indigenous churches and 25 mission churches.

The Muria synod is the oldest non-Western Mennonite church. It came into being in 1925 after several decades of mission work by European Mennonites, and since then has developed largely through the initiative and vision of lay leaders. In 1975 Mennonite Brethren Missions/Services was asked to supply resource people for the training of workers for the church's own mission agency, PIPKA. This cooperative arrangement has allowed the Mennonite Brethren to have a small part in the extension of the Muria churches on three of the major islands of Indonesia, and among a number of cultural and religious groups, including urban Muslims and jungle tribalists. (In 1984, according to PIPKA's plan, Missions/Services phased out its personnel involvement, except for periodic teaching visits. However, it continues a schedule of declining financial support.)

Sri Wandaningsih

Mrs. Sri Wandaningsih (Wanda) is from an Indonesian community heavily steeped in Javanese mysticism. Her family had always been very religious. According to Wanda, "We worshipped something—a spirit whom we could speak to—that was very great, very wonderful and very powerful. We called it God." Later, the spirit told Wanda that this great power was actually the souls of the dead of ancient times. Because her family had great respect for the ancient people, they came to believe that their souls were actually the soul of God.

"I learned about the spirits from my father," she says, recalling her childhood. "He did all sorts of strange things like bathing at seven different wells or in a mixture of water and flowers. He put various fetishes around our house and even on our bodies. Strings were tied around our necks, wrists and waists for protection.

"Since he was a mystic we believed that there was a spirit in him that could speak to us. I often went to him, worshipped him and talked with him. Sometimes I asked for help or for anything else that I needed. The spirit often talked about good things we believed to be of God." When she got to know her husband, she found that he also worshipped the spirits, and Wanda felt very fortunate to have a husband who knew God.

It seemed Wanda's family was in a good position in every area of life. Not only was her father a police colonel, but her

141

grandparents on both sides were members of the royal family. Her parents were well-to-do. She and her brothers and sisters had received a good education.

But discontent and doubt were building up, nevertheless. "Although my father was very powerful because of the spirits," Wanda says, "it seemed that when calamity struck, he couldn't do anything about it. He believed in one spirit, but there were all sorts of other spirits that could do him harm."

Indeed, the family's secure world began to fall apart. When Wanda was a youg woman her parents lost their financial security. Their relationship with each other suffered. Her mother suffered a serious heart attack and her father came down with acute diabetes. Her father did not feel fulfilled in his job. But above all, her father was losing some of his powers. Sometimes he could heal people, but other times he could not. That is when Wanda's doubts began to surface. Were these spirits really good? How could they be from God when they didn't make one's life happy?

One day she went with her husband to visit his guru. When they arrived, the guru warned her not to watch him while he was speaking. "I didn't know why he told me this," she says, "but then I noticed that his behavior was pretty strange. He would look upward and then stick out his tongue. What kind of spirit was this? When I asked him about it, he got angry and warned me again. If I watched what he was doing, it would cause doubt.

"He also warned me not to go into his front room, but for some reason I couldn't resist doing so. There on the wall was a drawing of the Javanese shadow puppets with some black writing around them. It seemed that this picture held some magical powers. Then suddenly, the guru came into the room and angrily chased me out. Why all the mystery? I wondered. I really had my doubts after that."

Her doubts moved her farther and farther away from her husband. As he spent more and more time away from home, they became strangers. Months later Wanda found out that for some time he had been involved with another woman and that he had gone so far as to marry her. "Looking back now," she reflects, "I know that my husband was bound by an evil spirit. That spirit took advantage of him and brought him into the worst things of life. I didn't find out about what had happened until almost a year after they were married. Now, I believe that God had actually closed my eyes and made me blind to what was going on until I was strong enough to accept it."

By the time Wanda found out, she had already heard the gospel, although her understanding of it was still limited. "When my husband came home," she says, "I suddenly felt a strong power not to be angry or accusing. I felt that he was the one who was really not strong enough to handle the situation." Shortly afterwards, they were formally divorced.

"My divorce was really a terrible time for me," she recalls. "My family had always been a good moral family and had avoided such scandals—and now, this very low thing had happened to me. Here in the East, young divorcees seem to be seen as the cause of a lot of trouble, and I didn't want anyone to blame me for anything. So I just didn't socialize. I stayed all closed up in the house except when I went to the university in the evenings to study English."

Through all of her misery, one positive influence was her younger brother, who had become a Christian long before the break-up. Disillusioned with the mysticism of his parents, and finding nothing attractive in Islam (Indonesia's main religion), he had found the answer to his spiritual quest in a Christian church. "I could see he had troubles too," Wanda says "but in spite of them all, he seemed happy. I knew this was because of his Christianity."

In the aftermath of her divorce, Wanda seriously began to search for God. "I went to the famous Hindu temples on the island of Bali, but I couldn't accept many of their strange ceremonies.

"I looked into Buddhism as well, and it taught about how

to love others. This part appealed to me, but I was really turned off by Buddhist austerity." Throughout her search, however, Wanda felt deep down that the Christians were the ones who really knew God. "It was only when I read the Bible that I was convinced I had found the truth. There was more there than just love. I got strength from every word. I started to know the one true God."

One day while at the dentist's office, a friend invited her to join an English class with Helen Nickel, a Mennonite Brethren missionary in Jakarta. There, to her suprise, the Bible was being used as a text. "Helen explained John 1:1 to us," Wanda relates, "and it all opened up for me. I decided to follow Christ. When Helen led me to the Lord, I knew I didn't have to doubt anymore, and I was happy."

"I wanted to grow in my faith," she continues, "and as I went deeper into studying the Bible, I learned more and more. God changed my life so wonderfully that suddenly I wasn't concerned about my own problems any more. As I began to teach English first in my own home and then later in an academy, I got my self-esteem back."

When Wanda became a Christian, another of her younger brothers who was living with her witnessed the change in her life and he often told her parents about it. One Saturday, the day of the Javanese New Year, a change took place in her father's life, too. According to his old belief, every New Year he had to meet with the spirit and sometimes have a special ceremony with flowers, water and eggs. This particular New Year, he was reluctant to do so.

When he told his son about it, the boy told him about the change in Wanda's life and suggested that her God must be the real one. This was the only living and redeeming God that Wanda's father had ever heard of and he suddenly realized that it was the only God who could free him from his struggles. For about 30 years, he had been bound by the spirits and now he wanted to give them up.

Since Wanda's father has become a Christian, there has

been a real change in his life. Upon retiring from the police force, he was able to get a job as a translator and has paid off his debts. The love between him and his wife has grown strong and they are no longer worried or burdened about their children. As Christians, they are secure in their faith in God.

What about the future? In recent years, Wanda has been translating devotional books for a Christian publishing company. She has also been installed as a church council member of the Muria Mennonite Church in Jakarta. What is the purpose of all this? She longs for others, including her former husband, to know God.

"I have never really worried about my future," she says, "I hope that I will be able to do right in the sight of God and learn to serve God by serving other people. I want so much to bring others to the Lord."

Carolyn Hamm

Yahya Chrismanto

Mr. Yahya Chrismanto speaks fondly of Jepara, a small town in Central Java, one of the main islands of Indonesia. He grew up there in a large family, the son of a business man who marketed the fine teak carvings for which the town is known.

Jepara reminds Chrismanto of the difficult decision he once had to make between family loyalties and obedience to Christ. As members of the minority group of Chinese which make up about four percent of Indonesia's total population, Chrismanto's parents transmitted to their children the Buddhist/Confucianist values of loyalty and honor, reverence for their ancestors and a submissive attitude toward their parents.

Chrismanto learned these lessons well, and they became very important to him. Also important, though, were the values he learned in the children's classes of the Muria Mennonite Church. His parents encouraged him to attend because, although they knew little about Christianity, they believed that it was good moral instruction for children. They didn't realize that for their son, it would be the beginning of a lengthy conflict.

Christianity came to Jepara in the 1930s through the extraordinary experience of a Chinese businessman, Mr. Tee Siem Tat. He had experienced a miraculous healing which led to his conversion. Soon afterwards, he came into contact with missionaries from South Russia whose name "Mennonite" he adopted when he founded the Muria Church in the 1920s. Through Mr. Tat's persistent witness and healing ministry, the gospel spread throughout the Chinese community, and branch congregations sprang up in seven cities and towns in Central Java.

The Muria children's classes were very attractive to Chrismanto. He says, "I loved to hear about Moses and Elijah and the prophets. At first I was attracted to the biblical characters because I was impressed by the miracles that happened. But later I realized that Jesus was different, greater than all the others. He had a task, a duty which he had to finish. I came to understand that he had to die for the sin of the world—for mine too."

Chrismanto was 13 when he decided to become a Christian. Although he wanted to explain and share his experience with his parents, he was held back by the Confucian tradition of ultimate respect for parents and ancestors. "So," he explains, "I communicated my message through good behavior."

When he was in junior high school, Chrismanto resolved to serve God the rest of his life. But he knew it wouldn't be easy. He explains, "when I finished high school I had a burden to go to seminary. At the same time I felt a burden for my parents because they worked hard to supply us with what we needed. I had a good reputation in school, often making top marks, so I was very hesitant. My parents wanted all their children to have a good education. They couldn't leave us an inheritance, they said, but they would give us the most important thing they could—an education."

After high school, Chrismanto entered the electronic engineering program in a university in Jakarta. During the gruesome years of 1965/66 his study was interrupted when an attempted Communist coup caused violence and political upheaval throughout Indonesia. "The country was very unstable," he recalls. "The university buildings were burned. It was a hard time, and there was much uncertainty."

147

In his parents' tradition, it would have been embarrassing and even dishonorable for Chrismanto to go back to his home town without finishing his studies. "At these crucial times," he says, "I prayed to the Lord for help in finishing my studies."

With the interruptions, the training which should have taken Chrismanto six or seven years, took twelve years to complete. He says, "During this time I had promised the Lord that if he helped me finish that degree, I would serve him full-time." But when he did graduate, he was in somewhat of a dilemma. After working so hard on his degree, how could he drop it all and go into full-time service? And how could he disappoint his parents who had worked so hard to support his needs?

The dilemma came to a head just a week after final exams, when Chrismanto came down with a serious illness. Confined to bed, he had time to think about the pleas of fellow Christians for him to serve the church. An important Muria leader, Andreas Setiawan had offered him the position of executive secretary for PIPKA, the mission arm of the Muria Church. Without considering it, he had instantly replied, "No." But a struggle had grown in him as other church members reminded him of his previous promise. Finally he had told them that he would serve God. "But," he said, "I need three years to work in the secular world first, to please my parents."

Now, on his sickbed he said the same thing to God. "Give me three years, then I will serve you full-time." But he felt God replying, "How do you even know if you will be alive in three years? What guarantee do you have? If your illness is serious, you could be gone in three months." In the end, peace came only when he decided to follow what he began to see as the will of God. He recovered from the illness, and shortly afterwards took up his leadership position with PIPKA, a position he still holds. Meanwhile, in 1967, his parents too decided to follow Christianity. Though it took some time, Chrismanto says that they eventually came to understand his decision to work for the church.

Chrismanto's concern to communicate the gospel and plant churches beyond the area where the Muria church was born is not new. Back in his student years, he was one of the small group of enthusiastic young people who in 1965 formed the first outreach of PIPKA in West Java. PIPKA worked to combat the views prevalent in the 1940s and '50s that the church should not expand beyond the Central Java area, and that the Muria Mennonite Church existed only for the ethnic Chinese.

He remembers how PIPKA was barely started when it was almost voted out of existence by the larger church. Reaching outside the Jepara area was regarded as simply too ambitious and expensive. Instead of giving up, however, the evangelistic leaders exhorted the church to consider what they called the "jeep in the garage plan": to look upon PIPKA as a worthy vehicle but one whose main problem was a lack of fuel. They insisted that it should be carefully "parked in a garage" for future use rather than dismantled.

In 1974, fuel to start the jeep was available because of PIPKA's contact with a representative of Mennonite Brethren Missions/Services who recommended that a working relationship be established.

Today there are 50 Indonesian missionaries working for PIPKA to establish mission churches in various areas of Indonesia. PIPKA now works to reach Muslim and tribal peoples in various parts of Java, and has even extended to the islands of Kalimantan and Sumatra. With a membership of about 7,000, the Muria Church now has 20 self-supporting churches, along with 27 mission churches begun by PIPKA (four of them self-supporting).

Chrismanto deeply respects his responsibilities—both toward the family into which he was born, and toward the family which he acquired as a born-again believer. His work as PIPKA'S Executive Secretary has become his central priority, although he is also a part-time pastor of a fast-growing branch church in Jakarta. ''The most encouraging thing in my work now,'' he says, ''is the support of the (Muria) churches for PIPKA. This is different from 5 or 10 years ago. The partial financial aid we received was an incentive, for we now can see that this work is not in vain. More are coming to agree that this work of evangelism is their duty, their responsibility. Our hope is to see more PIPKA congregations become adult churches—indigenous, mature.''

Frieda Esau

west germany

WEST GERMANY

Population: 61.6 million
Capital: Bonn
Language: German
Religions: Protestant (44%), Roman Catholic (45%).
(Evangelicals: 9%)

Mennonite Brethren Conference of Germany: 815 members in five churches and several satelite fellowships. (Congregations in Bavaria, southern Germany, are affiliated with the Austria MB conference.)
Missions/Services ministries: pastoral resource ministries, church planting

Common linguistic and cultural roots have made Germany a natural place for North American Mennonite Brethren mission work. Missions/Services ministries in the Neuwied and Neustadt areas grew out of Mennonite Central Committee refugee assistance following World War II, a program for fellow Mennonites leaving the Soviet Union. Since Missions/Services first entered the country in the early 1950s, a self-supporting conference has taken root, with churches in Neuwied, Neustadt, Lage, Bielefeld-Brakewede, and Bielefeld-Stieghorst.

A wave of Umsiedler (resettlers) from the Soviet Union during the 1970s helped swell the ranks of the churches, although many of them chose to remain independent. But the churches have also been active in reaching native Germans and are currently considering ways to reach Middle Eastern immigrant workers. Even foreign missions has figured prominently in the conference; the churches support missionaries in Brazil, Haiti and Spain, under several agencies.

Helmut Gareis

When Helmut Gareis of Traunreut, West Germany accepted Christ after a Traunreut Mennonite Brethren Church youth meeting in 1977, he didn't know that within just five years five members of his family would also decide for Jesus.

"The Bible says 'Believe in Christ and you and your house will be saved!'" says Helmut. "But I didn't think it would happen so quickly."

It all began in 1977 when Good News Corp workers John and Geri Warkentin, then of California, visited Helmut's high school English class to talk about life in their home state. Since Helmut had a sister living in California he was intrigued by John and Geri's comments; when they closed the lesson by inviting class members to a Traunreut Mennonite Brethren Church youth meeting, Helmut decided to attend in order to learn more about California life. He asked his sister Renate to join him.

"It was the first time I heard the gospel," says Helmut of the meeting. "It was very new and it touched me." Helmut and Renate enjoyed the meeting but Helmut wasn't sure that people could trust the Bible as completely as these Christian young people suggested.

"John Warkentin gave me a gospel of John," Helmut remembers, "and I decided to read it and then show John all the mistakes." But the Bible, he discovered, revealed the error of his ways. When he and Renate returned to the youth meeting Helmut was no longer interested in California life—he wanted to know more about the Christian life.

From John he learned that he needed to be forgiven and that he must ask Christ to become the Lord of his life. "At first I was reluctant to do so," Helmut shares, "because I had never heard about this kind of commitment before." After the meeting he went home and weighed the matter carefully. "I finally decided that if it was true—great. If it was wrong—nothing lost." In his room he quietly asked Christ to be his Savior.

"The moment I prayed all doubts about the decision vanished," he recalls. "I felt such joy inside and I knew I was saved."

His joy was multiplied when he learned that Renate had also decided to accept Christ. "I never gave much thought to God as a teenager," she remembers. "I only looked to him during emergencies—like before a high school exam."

Renate's decision to become a Christian was not based on the meeting's message—she admits that the discussion went "in and out"—but on the openness and friendliness of the young people. "The group members quickly became my friends," she recalls. "I decided that if God was good enough to give me such good friends that I wanted to give my life to Him."

Parents Willy and Erna soon noticed that something had happened to their children. "They were full of joy and peace," says Erna. Although religion had previously meant little to them they decided to find out why Helmut and Renate were suddenly attracted to God. Their first visit to the Traunreut Church was unsettling: "We had never before heard anyone preach like Lawrence Warkentin," she recalls.

Impressed by the change in her children she decided to study the Bible, beginning with Genesis. "I found it very hard to read," she says, "until Helmut suggested that I might be happier reading the Gospels."

For three years she and Willy attended services and

enjoyed a growing friendship with church-planting couple Lawrence and Selma Warkentin. One Sunday in 1980 Erna responded to a call for commitment and asked Christ into her life. Several weeks later, at Helmut's baptism, husband Willy also accepted Christ.

Renate, meanwhile, had moved to Munich in 1978 and while there met Gerhard Koenigeder. Gerhard, a small-town person in big-city Munich, was alone and friendless when he met a group of Christians doing street evangelism. After speaking with them for over an hour, he recalls that "something began to happen inside me. I felt that God could fill the emptiness I experienced while alone and away from home."

When he and Renate became close friends he began to visit the Traunreut Church with her. "I decided that I wanted what Renate, Helmut and her parents had," he says. Gerhard accepted Christ one year before their marriage in 1981.

After Gerhard's conversion, Renate excitedly wrote her sister in California: "Gerhard is saved," she wrote. "That's wonderful," her sister wrote back; "What is 'saved'?" In August, 1982 she phoned home to announce that she and her two children had accepted Jesus at a local California church. Erna still beams when she remembers the call.

In December, 1982 the Gareis family shared their new Christian joy with the Traunreut congregation when Erna, Renate and Gerhard were baptized. Willy was to be baptized sometime later, in 1983. The family is praying that the only family member who has not accepted Christ will do so in the near future.

In Bavaria, where few evangelical congregations have whole families attending services, the Gareis family is a testimony of God's love in action. "We are glad," says Helmut, "that our family can be a witness for our Lord."

John and Christine Longhurst

Gerda Retter

After accepting Christ in 1978, Gerda Retter of Erlinghausen, West Germany never doubted that her husband Hans would also come to faith. "What chance did I have?" he asks, noting that she prayed for him every day. "It was only a matter of time."

Religion was not a new idea for Gerda. Born into a Lutheran family and baptized as an infant, she was accustomed to attending church regularly. Although the Christianity she practiced was primarily tradition and ritual, she readily acknowledged the presence of a living God. As a young girl she often longed to be able to communicate with God, but the short, memorized prayers she was taught in Sunday school never seemed adequate.

"I recall hearing something about conversion once," Gerda says, "but I passed it off as irrelevant—I was already a member of the church." At times, however, she found herself wondering whether there wasn't more to Christianity.

For Hans, on the other hand, Christianity didn't even enter the picture. Heavily influenced by the anti-religious atmosphere of the Nazi regime, he was taught that the church and Christianity were outmoded traditions. "For me," he explains, "God was nature and nature was God—nothing more. I believed only what I could see."

Following their marriage in 1961, the Retters gradually sank into religious indifference. They set their sights on material goals—saving money, getting a raise, buying a home. For a time both were happy.

"It was enough for Hans," Gerda recalls, "but I began to wonder what lasting value there was in it." No longer convinced that religion could provide the answer she sought, Gerda began searching in other areas. "I studied yoga and psychic phenomena," she remembers, "but they gave me no satisfaction either."

Finding no real reason to live, her world grew darker and darker. For eight years she struggled with emotional and physical illnesses brought on by her lack of inner peace.

In June 1978 Gerda's two daughters brought home news about an evangelical tent campaign that was to be held in a nearby village. The girls were anxious to go and Gerda admitted being a little curious. Hans, however, wanted no part of it. "Go ahead if you want to," he said. "Just don't bother me about it."

Gerda was intrigued by what she heard at the meetings. "For the first time," she remembers, "I heard that if I lived apart from God I was lost. I also learned that God loved me, and wanted me to find salvation." But it was the message about occultism that really stirred her. "I saw clearly the darkness inside of me," she recalls. "I knew something had to change."

Without hesitation she got up from her seat, walked to the front and gave her life to Jesus. Her two daughters also made commitments that evening.

Upon their return home they excitedly began to share the good news with Hans. To their surprise he cut them off abruptly. "I don't want to know about it," he declared. "Don't bother me with that foolishness."

Although disappointed by his reaction, the trio refused to lose hope. "We began to pray for him every day," Gerda recalls. "We knew it would only be a matter of time."

Before leaving for family holidays that summer Gerda drew up lists of daily Bible readings and memory verses. As they travelled the family took turns reading the day's Bible passage. Each person was also responsible to memorize one verse a day. For the sake of family unity Hans decided to participate.

"I went along with them for the most part," he says. "Religion hadn't seemed to harm them any—in fact, there had been some positive changes. But I still felt that it wasn't for me."

In October, 1978 Gerda came into contact with another Christian in her village and together they organized a weekly house Bible study. Gerda enjoyed the opportunity to fellowship with other Christians and, as time passed, the little group began to grow in number.

Through the Bible study she learned of a special Easter service to be held at the nearby Brake Bible School. Since a number of others also wanted to attend, Hans was recruited to drive them. "They could have gone with someone else," he admits, "but to tell the truth, I was getting a little curious about Christianity. I decided it wouldn't hurt just to go along and see."

To his amazement he enjoyed every minute of the two-hour long program. "This whole atmosphere impressed me," he explains. "The singing was terrific and the preaching! I'd never heard such preaching before. The speakers were dynamic and outgoing. They really seemed to speak from their hearts."

To Gerda's surprise, Hans insisted on purchasing cassette recordings of the message. "I was even more shocked," she recalls, "when he began to play them over and over at home."

"Something was happening inside me," Hans explains. "I was beginning to feel that Christianity might have something to offer after all."

Gerda, encouraged by Hans' softening attitude to Christianity, decided to try to persuade him to go with her to a Mennonite Brethren church in the neighboring city of Lage. "I was becoming less and less satisfied with the fellowship

158

and training we were receiving at the State church," she explains. "I had heard good reports about the Mennonite church and was anxious to give it a try."

"She didn't need to try hard to convince me to go," Hans admits. "By this time I, too, was searching for the right answers."

The visit to the Lage church was an eye-opener for the whole family. "We couldn't get over how warm and friendly they were to us," Greda recalls. "It really felt as though they were glad we had come." While there they heard about an evangelistic campaign sponsored by the Lage church. This time, the whole family decided to attend. From the very first evening on, Gerda prayed fervently that the message of the Gospel would touch her husband's heart. When the invitation was given on the fourth evening, she was so engrossed in prayer that she failed to notice Hans quietly slip out of his chair and make his way forward. "When I opened my eyes, his chair was empty," she recalls. "I quickly looked forward and was overjoyed to see him kneeling at the front of the church."

"I knew even before we went that the time had come for me to make a decision," Hans says. "For the first three nights I just sat and listened. But by the fourth evening, I couldn't stay seated any longer."

Now that they had all made a decision for Christ, the Retters began to notice a marked difference in their family life. "Arguments and fights were common occurrences in our household," Gerda recalls. "We all had to be right. Communication would often break down for days. But now things are much gentler and quieter." "We're trying to learn patience," Hans agrees.

But the greatest changes have come in their relationships with the people they work with. "Most don't understand when I tell them I'm a committed Christian," Hans explains. "They look at me as though I'm some sort of super-holy fanatic." "The most frustrating thing," Gerda adds, "is that

159

they don't take us seriously."

"But," she continues, "when they have problems, we're the ones they talk to. It's our advice they want."

The Lage Mennonite Brethren church continues to play an important role in their lives. Baptized into membership in October 1981, they enjoy the support they feel from other Christians. "It's great to have a strong church behind us," Hans says. "We know we can go to them with our problems."

"I wouldn't want to be without it," Gerda adds.

As they look back, Hans and Gerda can see God's hand in their lives. "I'm so thankful for the way He has led us," Hans says. "I can't imagine living without Him."

John and Christine Longhurst

Lothar
and Ingrid
Setzphand

Lothar Stezphand, 45, has been a Christian only since July 1982. Together with his wife Ingrid and daughter Andrea, he attends the evangelical church in Stranberg, West Germany, just outside of Munich. The church, pastored by Henry and Helen Warkentin of Missions/Services, is an affiliated member of the Austrian Mennonite Brethren conference.

Sitting in his home just outside of Starnberg, Lothar related his journey to God. "I was reading the Psalms one day," he began," "and happened to come across Psalm 107:17-22. I was amazed. Those verses are like a condensed version of my own conversion story."

Picking up his Bible, he turned to the passage and began to read. "Fools, because of their rebellious way, and because of their iniquities, werc afflicted. Their souls abhorred all kinds of food, they drew near to the gates of death."

"I had known for a long time that something was missing in my life," he continued. "There was a feeling of emptiness that I could never seem to fill. My work as a chemical engineer placed me under a great deal of stress. We were always busy and under pressure. Upon arrival home at night I would usually have to relax in front of the TV with a beer.

"On several occasions I actually became physically ill from the emotional strain. I finally concluded that this just couldn't be the right way to live and I began to look for a solution.

"I thought I had three options: Quit my job and look for another that wasn't as stressful. Or I could bury myself in hobbies, like gardening or painting. Finally, I could keep working at my job for ten more years and then retire. We could sell our home, buy a cheaper one and with the difference live peacefully for the rest of our lives.

"But as I thought about the three options, I realized that they wouldn't solve my inner emptiness. Mine was an emotional problem, and physical remedies just weren't going to help.

"Around this time a nearby family invited us over for a visit. Since I knew they were Christians and attended a small church not far from our home, I was interested to learn more about what they believed. We accepted the invitation.

"I was surprised at the ease of conversation we enjoyed— I was able to tell them how I was feeling. They, in turn, shared how they had become Christians and what their church was all about. I also learned that they believed in life after death. This was an entirely new concept for me. My upbringing and university education had taught me to trust only things that could be seen and touched. What couldn't be proved was unbelievable.

"But something inside me wouldn't let me dismiss the possibility of life after death. I felt there must be more. A real conflict began inside—a battle between my philosophy of realism and my feelings.

"Looking for answers, I later attended an evangelistic meeting at the Word of Life retreat center near our home. The speaker was the American astronaut, James Irwin. I was impressed; something seemed to radiate from him as he spoke. He talked about problems he experienced before becoming a Christian. To my surprise, they were identical to the problems I was having. But even though I knew he was right, something inside resisted. I told myself as I left, 'We'll see about this. It needs time to settle.'

"Shortly after, another family from the church invited us

to a Christian Business Association dinner. We sat with a Christian doctor, and both Ingrid and I liked him instinctively. When he spoke to us of faith it went right to our hearts. After the dinner he invited us to a Christian Businessmen's weekend seminar. We decided to go.

"While driving there I realized the time had come to make a decision. Yet all that weekend the struggle continued. 'Go ahead, decide for Christ' said one voice. 'Don't do it! You'll be embarrassed,' said another. But as I struggled I made two important decisions. First, that I had to forget these doubts and just trust God and, second, that I had to trust God now. I might not get another chance."

Reaching for his Bible, Lothar read again from the Psalm.

"Then they cried out to the Lord in their trouble; he saved them out of their distresses. He sent his word and healed them, and delivered them from their destructions."

"It was near the end of the weekend. Both Ingrid and I knew that the time had come. We stood up in front of the group—my heart was beating furiously—and prayed, asking God to forgive us and make us his children. When we had finished a feeling of freedom came over me. It was overwhelming! People embraced us, crying; I couldn't understand why they cared. It was my problem, not theirs. But now I understand!

"The time after my conversion was very full of emotion. I needed time to stabilize. One of the first things I realized was that the devil doesn't stop just because you decide for Christ. During that first week, the devil spoke to me at every turn, using all the philosophical arguments I had been taught: 'Don't go through with this, it's all foolishness. Just forget it, and get on with your life.'

"I soon realized that I needed to immerse myself in God's Word and remain in communication with Him through prayer. The warm accepting fellowship at the Starnberg church was a real encouragement as well. It was almost like coming into paradise! We could go to those people with any problem and know that they'd care about us and try to help.

"As far as work was concerned, I don't think I can point to any drastic changes. I went, rather, through a series of phases. The first phase occurred just after I made my decision for Christ. All I could think about was Christianity. I forgot all about the tension and stress of my job. Unfortunately, that only lasted a few weeks.

"The second phase was much more difficult. In addition to the return of normal job stress I now felt a double tension, wishing so badly that Christianity would solve this problem. I didn't want to have to give it up as a failure.

"But fortunately there was a third stage, the one I'm in now. The tension and stress I feel at work is not completely gone, but I feel much more relaxed. I know I haven't found the solution, but I'm confident that I'm heading in the right direction.

"One of my greatest joys is that we have come to the Lord as a family; our daughter Andrea also accepted Christ this past summer. It's a real privilege to have Bible study together. I also realize more and more that in order to grow in faith I must take time to listen to God. Not only that, I must be willing to hear what He has to say to me. Otherwise I won't be able to grow. Mennonite Brethren missionaries Henry and Helen Warkentin have been a great help in this area. They've both really encouraged us in our Christian lives.

"In the past life was so boring. I tried so hard to fill time. Now it seems as though 24 hours isn't nearly enough! I can't fit in everything I'd like to do. For me that is a tremendous change. Before I needed beer to settle myself down and dull reality. Now I want none of it. I want my mind clear to read and think. I wasn't forced to stop doing any of these things. The changes came naturally.

"I now look forward to the future. Sure, there will be times of uncertainty and fear, but I no longer worry about what will come. I know God will lead step by step."

Turning to his Bible once again, Lothar read the remaining verses;

"Let them give thanks to the Lord for His loving kindness, and for His wonders to the sons of men! Let them also offer sacrifices of thanksgiving, and tell of His works with joyful singing."

John and Christine Longhurst

austria

AUSTRIA

Population:	7.6 million
Capital:	Vienna
Language:	German
Religions:	Roman Catholic (85%), Lutheran. (Evangelicals: 0.5%)

Mennonite Brethren Conference of Austria (includes Bavaria, West Germany): 254 members, 7 churches, 4 mission posts.

Missions/Services ministries: pastoral, evangelistic; leadership resource

Mennonite Brethren church planting in Austria followed on the heels of the disruption of World War II. It began with an evangelistic team among refugees in the Linz area in 1952. New believers were soon organized into a fellowship, which became a church in 1955. Natural contacts led to other worship groups in Steyr, Wels, Salzburg and Vienna. Outreach points in Amstetten, Liezen and Braunau have been added more recently, with Liezen incorporating as a church in 1984.

The Austrian conference, which includes churches in the German province of Bavaria, continues to rely heavily on the missionary team for pastoral and church planting ministries, although several ordained and lay leaders are serving faithfully. The churches are currently working with other evangelicals in beginning a joint Bible school in Austria.

Linda Schrattenecker

Linda Schrattenecker's conversion is a story of losing and finding. In 1970 she lost a son. Six years later, she found a Father.

Linda was born in Salzburg, Austria, to devout Roman Catholic parents. She attended Mass regularly as a child and, as she grew older, was careful to fulfill all obligations demanded by the church.

Following her marriage, Linda prayed fervently that she would be able to raise her only child into a God-fearing young man. As her son grew older, it appeared as though she had been successful.

While away at university, however, the son came into contact with a group of Moonies, followers of Sun Myung Moon of South Korea. He joined the sect and, after only a few months' involvement, dropped out of university and left Austria for a Moonie community in the United States.

Linda's world fell in. Desperate, she turned to prayer, using her rosary over and over. For days she continued, but received no answer. She felt as though God were dead.

As her desperation grew, Linda made plans for a pilgrimage to the Italian burial place of St. Antonio, hoping that he, the patron saint of lost possessions, would be able to intercede to God on her behalf.

Upon arrival at the shrine she found hundreds of people ahead of her, all waiting in line for a chance to touch the marble coffin. Those closest were clutching at the tomb, crying and wailing as they begged for intercession.

The scene dismayed and sickened Linda; she knew this couldn't be the right way to God. In despair she screamed aloud: "Please God! Show me the right way to find my son." But there was no answer. Discouraged, Linda returned to Austria.

One day shortly after her return home, she felt an urge to get out of the house. She strolled to a store near her home and, upon exiting, walked past the only car in the parking lot. She stopped short when she read a sticker on the rear window: "If your God is dead, try mine—Jesus lives."

Excited, Linda ran back into the store, frantically asking everyone in sight if they knew who owned the car. No one could tell her, so she ran back to the car and waited.

A few minutes later a young man, his arms full of shopping bags, left the store and came to the car. "Is this your car?" Linda asked. "Yes," he replied. "Can you explain what this means?" she queried, pointing to the sticker. "It means that Jesus is alive—he lives in my heart," the man responded. As they talked together, Linda shared the story of her son, and her search for answers.

When they parted he asked if he could come visit her. Linda agreed and they arranged to meet some morning that week.

For three days Linda sat at home, waiting for the doorbell to ring. Finally, on the fourth morning, he appeared, a book under his arm.

When she poured out her questions, he took the book—a Bible—and read different verses. Linda was disappointed. She had expected a formula of some kind: "Do this and this, and you'll get your son back."

Nevertheless, she was intrigued by the visitor's openness and friendliness. They met several more times and a real friendship developed. The young man—a Mennonite Brethren church worker named Reinhold Buxbaum—invited her to attend Bible studies and church services at the Mennonite Brethren church in Salzburg. Linda went and, to her amazement, enjoyed herself. The people took a real interest in her, and as she continued to attend often mentioned that they were praying for her.

One afternoon Linda was invited to the Buxbaums' home. Another church worker from North America was also there, and during the course of the conversation asked Linda if she was a child of God. "I don't know," Linda replied honestly. "Then let's pray about it," the church worker responded.

And so they all began to pray—one by one around the table. Linda was afraid; she had never prayed out loud in a group before. But when her turn came, something suddenly overcame her and she began to pray, pouring out her heart and soul. The others around the table wept as Linda committed her life to God.

Linda's conversion took place in 1976. In the years since then her son has not returned home, but Linda feels that their relationship through letters is improving. More important, she is no longer without hope. "My life is different now," she explains. "I have found a living Father, and through Him I have hope and peace."

John and Christine Longhurst

Alois Metz

For many Germans and Austrians, the presence of Turkish guest workers in their countries is a problem that they wish would, quite literally, go away. But for Alois Metz of Steyr, Austria, the Turks aren't a problem—they're an opportunity. "I think the Lord has sent them to us," says the young salesman who spends his spare time visiting and distributing Christian literature to the foreigners.

Turks began coming to Germany, Austria and other western European countries when manpower shortages threatened to stall economic recovery after World War II. Recruited to perform unskilled jobs that Europeans considered onerous and menial, they were welcomed as guests.

Since they weren't expected to stay long, virtually nothing was done to integrate them into life in Germany or Austria. Integration was, in fact, viewed as detrimental; it would make their eventual return home more difficult. As a result, the over 1.2 million Turks in Germany have retained their distinct cultural identity. It's much the same for the over 166,000 Turks in Austria.

Some Turks went home, but most stayed. Their presence wasn't a problem until both the German and Austrian economies suffered setbacks during the recent global recession, which sent unemployment rates on an upward swing. The Turks, once actively recruited to fill manpower shortages, were now considered unnecessary. According to recent surveys 66 percent of Germans and 70 percent of Austrians simply wish they would go home. Attitudes like these lend a sense of urgency to Metz's ministry. "If they are forced to go home," he states, "many will return with empty hearts because Christians have not given them the gospel." Since 1982 he has carried a special burden for Turkish guest workers. After work he goes down to the poorer part of Steyr, where the Turks live, and visits them in their homes and coffee-bars.

Metz himself has been a Christian only since 1976. "My journey to Christ began after I saw the movie *Jesus Christ Superstar*," he shares. "The hammer blows stayed with me long after the movie—'If Christ endured such pain for me,' I asked myself, 'then shouldn't I take him more seriously?'" He later went to see the movie *Jonathan Livingstone Seagull*. "It convinced me that there was another life and a heaven beyond life on earth," he recalls.

Conversion came when he heard the story of the prodigal son on the radio one evening. "As I listened I realized that God loved me, that I was lost. I realized that God, just like the father in the story, wanted to welcome me home with open arms." He joined the Steyr M.B. Church later that same year.

1979 to 1982 found him at Bible school in Switzerland, where he first received his burden for Turks. "I really knew nothing about them," he shares, "but my first contact attracted me to them." He especially loves the Turkish children. "You should see them," he says with obvious delight. Upon return to Steyr he began making new friends among the Turkish community. "It isn't hard to become friends with them," he says. "In a country where so many people dislike them, they are open to an Austrian who wants to be a friend."

Metz is convinced that God has brought Turks to Austria and Germany for a purpose. "It is very difficult for missionaries to go to Turkey," he shares. "So God sent the Turks to us." On the other hand, he adds sadly, "Christians in Europe

173

have not caught the potential of this tremendous opportunity."

He admits that language is the greatest barrier to evangelism among the Turks. Most European Christians have not, moreover, had experience in evangelism among Muslims. "Witnessing to them is never easy," says Metz, "but it gets easier as your love for them grows."

John and Christine Longhurst

Joseph Puehringer

It isn't difficult to understand why Joseph Puehringer of Linz, Austria became an alcoholic before the age of 20.

A severe inferiority complex, the result of a harelip, a deformed left hand and his parents' divorce, caused him to retreat into bitter self-resignation and loneliness. "My whole life centered around myself and my handicaps," Joseph recalls. "All I could see was my own inadequacy. As a result my problems continued to grow until I couldn't face them anymore."

Living alone and without friends, Joseph turned to the only solution he knew: alcohol. "I tried to drown my problems by becoming hopelessly drunk," he recalls. In order to support his drinking habits, he turned to stealing. Caught on a number of occasions, he spent over a year in prison.

Fortunately, Joseph's story does not end there. "When I look back now," he says, "I can see how God cared for and sought after me."

Joseph's first contact with Christianity came in an unexpected manner. As a member of a local book club he was obliged to make a minimum of four purchases a year. On one occasion he had difficulty choosing a book but happened to notice that the club also sold Bibles. "I figured I might as well buy a Bible," he recalls, "since I had to buy something."

The Bible was placed on a shelf in his apartment and, for the most part, Joseph forgot that he owned it. But on occasions when problems overwhelmed him, he would involuntarily reach for it, searching its pages for a solution.

But a solution never came. "I would try hard to read the Bible," he recalls. "But I could never seem to make sense of it."

One hot summer afternoon in 1980 Joseph decided that the last thing he wanted to do was to have another meal alone in his cramped apartment. On impulse he walked downtown to buy himself some supper. While crossing the main city square he noticed a young man handing out literature. When Joseph was given a piece he merely glanced at it and walked on.

"What do you think about God?" the young man called after him. "Have you ever heard about Jesus Christ?" Joseph turned. "I'm not interested," he replied. "I have enough problems as it is. The last thing I need is God. Besides, I can take care of myself."

"You're wrong," the young man responded. "You'll never be able to solve your problems until you accept Jesus as your Savior."

The man's reply caught Joseph's attention and, forgetting all about supper, he turned back to hear more. When the young man invited him to a Christian coffeehouse nearby, he quickly accepted, eager to learn how he could deal with his many problems.

Joseph was fascinated by the music and testimonies he heard that evening. "Everything that was said or sung revolved around Jesus," he recalls. "This was something entirely new for me." Following the presentation he became involved in a discussion with a number of performers. Many of his questions about God came to the surface and Joseph was surprised to find that these people had answers.

As the evening came to a close everyone present joined together for a time of prayer. "I was amazed," Joseph remembers. "They actually spoke as if God was present." He enjoyed the prayer time and found himself wishing he could talk to God in the same way.

Joseph was one of the last people to leave the coffeehouse that evening. After locking the doors, one of the members asked, "Will we see you again tomorrow night?" "Oh, I don't know," he replied casually, feigning indifference. "Perhaps I'll drop in if I have time."

But even as he walked home that evening, Joseph knew he would never be the same. "I went to bed," he says, "but there was no way I could sleep. The evening's conversation kept running through my mind, over and over. I tossed and turned the whole night."

The coffeehouse was still on his mind when he arose the next morning. "I realized that if I didn't make a decision for Christ today, I might never get another chance."

He spent the entire day in anticipation of the evening, and even before the coffeehouse opened, was waiting in front of the doors. As the workers began to arrive, Joseph shared with them his desire to accept Christ. Surprised and overjoyed, they were only too eager to help.

Since making that decision, Joseph has become a new person. Previously unable to look others in the eye, he is now anxious to meet new people and tell of God's work in his life. Joseph also appreciates the fellowship and acceptance he finds at the Linz Mennonite Brethren church. He was baptized there in March, 1982.

"You know," he says, "That young man was right. I wasn't able to solve my problems without Christ. What a tremendous difference Jesus has made in my life."

John and Christine Longhurst

spain

SPAIN

Population: 38.3 million
Capital: Madrid
Language: Spanish
Religion: Roman Catholic (99%). (Evangelicals: 0.4%)

Mennonite Brethren Church of Spain: 10 members, two worship groups
Missions/Services ministries: church planting (evangelistic Bible studies, youth activities, public rallies, etc.)

Missions/Services entered Madrid in 1976 to evangelize and plant churches among high-rise apartment dwellers in the northern part of the city. Since then the Missions/Services team has established two Bible centers in the Bellas Vistas and Saconia neighborhoods. These have been bases for fellowship as well as evangelistic English and crafts classes, children's clubs and gospel film showings. While baptism and church membership has been slow in coming, much seed-sowing has taken place since 1976, and strong relationships have been established.

Antonio Alvaro

Choosing a church was never a problem when Antonio Alvaro was a young boy; there only was one legal choice.

"I attended the Roman Catholic church," says the 21-year-old audio technician, "but I didn't know anything about Christ. All I knew was what we were taught in our religion classes. There we learned about the traditions and rituals of the Catholic church. But these didn't lead us to Christ."

The Spain into which Antonio was born believed that to be a Spaniard meant to be Catholic. Under General Francisco Franco's regime Catholicism was named the official state religion. The government attempted to destroy all signs of evangelicalism through persecution and imprisonment.

The late 1960s saw a gradual growth of religious tolerance and, even before Franco's death in 1975, the country opened up to evangelical influences. Mennonite Brethren Missions/Services came to Spain in 1976.

Antonio's initial contact with Mennonite Brethren in Madrid occurred soon afterwards. A poster advertising an upcoming film series at the Saconia Bible Center caught his attention and, together with a group of friends, he decided to attend. The film was followed by a short talk and when the invitation was given to accept Christ, a number of young people raised their hands. Antonio was one of them. "I had so much to learn," Antonio says of his early decision. "I had to start right at the beginning. This was a true knowledge of Jesus."

Antonio maintained contact with the Bible Center in Saconia. He attended English classes offered there and, with a group of friends, participated in youth activities. Later he got to know new missionaries to Spain, exchanging advice about Spanish for help with his English.

At present Antonio is involved in one-on-one Bible studies with Misions/Services worker Ron Penner. "Antonio is something special," says Penner. "Out of all the young people who raised their hands that night, he's the only one who has stuck it out."

"But," Antonio admits, "it's not been an easy decision. After my initial experiences I've gone through a series of highs and lows—good and bad times."

The step Antonio finds hardest to take is baptism. Even though Catholicism ceased to be Spain's official religion in 1979, it still exerts a powerful influence over the Spanish people. The Roman Catholic church is so closely tied to the country's history and culture that for many, to cease being a Catholic is to become less of a Spaniard.

Antonio's hesitancy about baptism stems not so much from the fact that it severs all ties with Catholicism, but rather from a fear of broken relationships with family and friends who don't understand.

Antonio is especially afraid for his mother. "Her friends will not understand," he says. "And she will not be able to explain why I left the church."

But despite these difficult decisions, Antonio is continuing to grow. "My faith has given me a real sense of peace and security," he says. "It is really helping me."

Only recently, through the example of another new Christian, Antonio discovered that the Christian life was a dynamic and vital day-to-day experience of commitment. "I realized that accepting Christ into my heart is not enough—I must do something about it every day."

Confident in his growing faith, and grateful for the influence of Missions/Services workers in his own life, Antonio feels positive about future work in Madrid. "I know we will be able to accomplish many things with the help of our Lord."

John and Christine Longhurst

Cipriano
Campanero

'' 'Faithful' is the word I would use to describe Cipriano Campanero,'' says Ron Penner, Missions/Services worker in Madrid. Co-worker Ruth Klassen agrees. "Cipriano's dedicated Bible reading is an example to the entire church.''

Cipriano, who serves as president of the Mennonite Brethren community in Spain, cannot recall a single day since his conversion four years ago when he has failed to spend time with the Scriptures. "If anything," he says, "it's even more important to me now than when I first believed.''

Born in the 1930s during the Spanish Civil War, Cipriano grew up in a country which boasted one political party and one legal religion. Under the dictatorship of General Francisco Franco, Roman Catholicism was declared the official religion of Spain.

"I was baptized into the Catholic Church as an infant," Cipriano recalls, "and attended Mass with my family.'' His early schooling and catechism classes gave him exposure to the Bible but, he admits, "I was never really interested. I considered myself a good Roman Catholic, but nothing was happening deep inside me.''

Economic concerns forced Cipriano to leave school at 14 and enter the working world. During this time he drifted further away from the Catholic Church. "I was living my life only for myself—I had very little interest in spiritual things.''

"But," he says, recalling those many years of spiritual indifference, "my conscience gave me no peace." On his 40th birthday he remarked to his wife, "The years are passing and we are not attending church."

Through a Christian co-worker he received a Bible and began to read it regularly. He was also given a copy of Billy Graham's book, *Peace with God*, which he read through a number of times, carefully looking up every Scripture reference. "I came to see the promise of God and salvation through the death of Christ," he recalls. "I knelt down, asked God to forgive my sins, and invited Christ into my life."

A Bible correspondence course brought him into contact with the Saconia Mennonite Brethren Bible Center in Madrid. He began attending the Tuesday evening Bible studies, and soon made the Center his church home.

"My personal Bible study is very important to me," he explains. "It's my spiritual food, the guide for my life. But I also enjoy studying the Bible with fellow believers. There I can see the depth and variety of understanding in other Christians."

Despite his full-time work as a cabinet maker with an electronics firm outside Madrid, Cipriano finds time to serve as lay leader in the Saconia Bible Center. "He really takes leadership seriously," says Penner. "He's always willing to help; we've really learned to count on Cipriano."

And he does help, in ways that range from sorting out the legal difficulties involved in the 1981 purchase of a second Bible center to playing harmonica for special music on Sunday morning. "Cipriano gives leadership just by his example," says Ruth Klassen. "He is always very supportive and affirming."

Cipriano is also committed to a vision for the larger Spanish Church. "The evangelical church in Spain must come alive," he says. "We must be on fire for Christ." He prays that God will unite Spanish Christians and help them to work alongside missionaries in a seed-planting ministry.

For this reason Cipriano is never hesitant about his

witness to others. He readily shares his testimony, and enjoys preparing messages based on his study of the Word.

"We must share the Good News with others," he says. "We don't study God's Word just so that we can be nourished, but so that we will be able to nourish others."

John and Christine Longhurst